# RESUMES
# FOR
# HEALTH
# AND
# MEDICAL
# CAREERS

**Professional Resumes Series**

# RESUMES
# FOR
# HEALTH
# AND
# MEDICAL
# CAREERS

## The Editors of
## VGM Career Horizons

*Printed on recyclable paper*

 **VGM Career Horizons**
a division of *NTC Publishing Group*
Lincolnwood, Illinois USA

# ACKNOWLEDGMENT

The editors gratefully acknowledge Martha Eberts and Jeffrey S. Johnson for their help in the writing and production of this book.

**Library of Congress Cataloging-in-Publication Data**

Resumes for health & medical careers/the editors of VGM Career Horizons

    p.       cm.—(VGM professional resumes series)

ISBN 0-8442-4154-7
  1. Résumés (Employment)  2. Medical personnel—Vocational guidance.  I. VGM Career Horizons (Firm)  II. Title: Resumes for health and medical careers.  III. Series: VGM's professional resumes series.
  [DNLM: 1. Health Occupations.  2. Job Application.  W 21 R436 1993]
R690.R48  1993
808'.06665—dc20
DNLM/DLC                          92-48533
for Library of Congress               CIP

1996 Printing

# CONTENTS

Introduction     vii

*Chapter One*
**The Elements of a Good Resume**     1

*Chapter Two*
**Writing Your Resume**     15

*Chapter Three*
**Assembly and Layout**     19

*Chapter Four*
**The Cover Letter**     27

*Chapter Five*
**Sample Resumes**     29

*Chapter Six*
**Sample Cover Letters**     131

# INTRODUCTION

Your resume is your first impression on a prospective employer. Though you may be articulate, intelligent, and charming in person, a poor resume may prevent you from ever having the opportunity to demonstrate your interpersonal skills, because a poor resume may prevent you from ever being called for an interview. While few people have ever been hired solely on the basis of their resume, a well-written, well-organized resume can go a long way toward helping you land an interview. Your resume's main purpose is to get you that interview. The rest is up to you and the employer. If you both feel that you are right for the job and the job is right for you, chances are you will be hired.

A resume must catch the reader's attention yet still be easy to read and to the point. Resume styles have changed over the years. Today, brief and focused resumes are preferred. No longer do employers have the patience, or the time, to review two or three pages of solid type. A resume should be only one page long, if possible, and never more than two pages. Time is a precious commodity in today's business world and the resume that is concise and straightforward will usually be the one that gets noticed.

Let's not make the mistake, though, of assuming that writing a brief resume means that you can take less care in preparing it. A successful resume takes time and thought, and if you are willing to make the effort, the rewards are well worth it. Think of your resume as a sales tool with the product being you. You want to sell yourself to a prospective employer. This book is designed to help you prepare a resume that will help you further your career—to land that next job, or first job, or to return to the work force after years of absence. So, read on. Make the effort and reap the rewards that a strong resume can bring to your career. Let's get to it!

# Chapter One

# THE ELEMENTS OF A GOOD RESUME

*A* winning resume is made of the elements that employers are most interested in seeing when reviewing a job applicant. These basic elements are the essential ingredients of a successful resume and become the actual sections of your resume. The following is a list of elements that may be used in a resume. Some are essential; some arc optional. We will be discussing these in this chapter in order to give you a better understanding of each element's role in the makeup of your resume:

1. Heading
2. Objective
3. Work Experience
4. Education
5. Honors
6. Activities
7. Certificates and Licenses
8. Professional Memberships
9. Special Skills
10. Personal Information
11. References

The first step in preparing your resume is to gather together information about yourself and your past accomplishments. Later you will refine this information, rewrite it in the most effective language, and organize it into the most attractive layout. First, let's take a look at each of these important elements individually.

# Heading

The heading may seem to be a simple enough element in your resume, but be careful not to take it lightly. The heading should be placed at the top of your resume and should include your name, home address, and telephone numbers. If you can take calls at your current place of business, include your business number, since most employers will attempt to contact you during the business day. If this is not possible, or if you can afford it, purchase an answering machine that allows you to retrieve your messages while you are away from home. This way you can make sure you don't miss important phone calls. *Always* include your phone number on your resume. It is crucial that when prospective employers need to have immediate contact with you, they can.

# Objective

When seeking a particular career path, it is important to list a job objective on your resume. This statement helps employers know the direction that you see yourself heading, so that they can determine whether your goals are in line with the position available. The objective is normally one sentence long and describes your employment goals clearly and concisely. See the sample resumes in this book for examples of objective statements.

The job objective will vary depending on the type of person you are, the field you are in, and the type of goals you have. It can be either specific or general, but it should always be to the point.

In some cases, this element is not necessary, but usually it is a good idea to include your objective. It gives your possible future employer an idea of where you are coming from and where you want to go.

The objective statement is better left out, however, if you are uncertain of the exact title of the job you seek. In such a case, the inclusion of an overly specific objective statement could result in your not being considered for a variety of acceptable positions; you should be sure to incorporate this information in your cover letter, instead.

# Work Experience

This element is arguably the most important of them all. It will provide the central focus of your resume, so it is necessary that this section be as complete as possible. Only by examining your work experience in depth can you get to the heart of your accomplishments and present them in a way that demonstrates the strength of your qualifications. Of course, someone just out of school will have less work experience than someone who has been working for a number of years, but the amount of information isn't the most important thing—rather, how it is presented and how it highlights you as a person and as a worker will be what counts.

As you work on this section of your resume, be aware of the need for accuracy. You'll want to include all necessary information about each of your jobs, including job title, dates, employer, city, state, responsibilities, special projects, and accomplishments. Be sure to only list company accomplishments for which you were directly responsible. If you haven't participated in any special projects, that's all right—this area may not be relevant to certain jobs.

The most common way to list your work experience is in *reverse chronological order*. In other words, start with your most recent job and work your way backwards. This way your prospective employer sees your current (and often most important) job before seeing your past jobs. Your most recent position, if the most important, should also be the one that includes the most information, as compared to your previous positions. If you are just out of school, show your summer employment and part-time work, though in this case your education will most likely be more important than your work experience.

The following worksheets will help you gather information about your past jobs.

## WORK EXPERIENCE
### Job One:

Job Title _____

Dates _____

Employer _____

City, State _____

Major Duties _____

_____

_____

_____

_____

_____

_____

Special Projects _____

_____

_____

_____

Accomplishments _____

_____

_____

_____

_____

_____

_____

_____

_____

**Job Two:**

Job Title _____

Dates _____

Employer _____

City, State _____

Major Duties _____

_____

_____

_____

_____

_____

_____

_____

Special Projects _____

_____

_____

_____

Accomplishments _____

_____

_____

_____

_____

_____

_____

_____

_____

**Job Three:**

Job Title _____

Dates _____

Employer _____

City, State _____

Major Duties _____

_____

_____

_____

_____

_____

_____

Special Projects _____

_____

_____

_____

Accomplishments _____

_____

_____

_____

_____

_____

_____

_____

**Job Four:**

Job Title _____

Dates _____

Employer _____

City, State _____

Major Duties _____

_____

_____

_____

_____

_____

_____

Special Projects _____

_____

_____

_____

Accomplishments _____

_____

_____

_____

_____

_____

_____

_____

_____

# Education

Education is the second most important element of a resume. Your educational background is often a deciding factor in an employer's decision to hire you. Be sure to stress your accomplishments in school with the same finesse that you stressed your accomplishments at work. If you are looking for your first job, your education will be your greatest asset, since your work experience will most likely be minimal. In this case, the education section becomes the most important. You will want to be sure to include any degrees or certificates you received, your major area of concentration, any honors, and any relevant activities. Again, be sure to list your most recent schooling first. If you have completed graduate-level work, begin with that and work in reverse chronological order through your undergraduate education. If you have completed an undergraduate degree, you may choose whether to list your high school experience or not. This should be done only if your high school grade-point average was well above average.

The following worksheets will help you gather information for this section of your resume. Also included are supplemental worksheets for honors and for activities. Sometimes honors and activities are listed in a section separate from education, most often near the end of the resume.

## EDUCATION

School _____

Major or Area of Concentration _____

Degree _____

Date _____

School _____

Major or Area of Concentration _____

Degree _____

Date _____

# Honors

Here, you should list any awards, honors, or memberships in honorary societies that you have received. Usually these are of an academic nature, but they can also be for special achievement in sports, clubs, or other school activities. Always be sure to include the name of the organization honoring you and the date(s) received. Use the worksheet below to help gather your honors information.

**HONORS**

Honor: _____

Awarding Organization: _____

Date(s): _____

Honor: _____

Awarding Organization: _____

Date(s): _____

Honor: _____

Awarding Organization: _____

Date(s): _____

Honor: _____

Awarding Organization: _____

Date(s): _____

# Activities

You may have been active in different organizations or clubs during your years at school; often an employer will look at such involvement as evidence of initiative and dedication. Your ability to take an active role, and even a leadership role, in a group should be included on your resume. Use the worksheet provided to list your activities and accomplishments in this area. In general, you should exclude any organization the name of which indicates the race, creed, sex, age, marital status, color, or nation of origin of its members.

## ACTIVITIES

Organization/Activity: _____

Accomplishments: _____

_____

_____

Organization/Activity: _____

Accomplishments: _____

_____

_____

Organization/Activity: _____

Accomplishments: _____

_____

_____

Organization/Activity: _____

Accomplishments: _____

_____

_____

As your work experience increases through the years, your school activities and honors will play less of a role in your resume, and eventually you will most likely only list your degree and any major honors you received. This is due to the fact that, as time goes by, your job performance becomes the most important element in your resume. Through time, your resume should change to reflect this.

## Certificates and Licenses

The next potential element of your resume is certificates and licenses. You should list these if the job you are seeking requires them and you, of course, have acquired them. If you have applied for a license, but have not yet received it, use the phrase "application pending."

License requirements vary by state. If you have moved or you are planning to move to another state, be sure to check with the appropriate board or licensing agency in the state in which you are applying for work to be sure that you are aware of all licensing requirements.

Always be sure that all of the information you list is completely accurate. Locate copies of your licenses and certificates and check the exact date and name of the accrediting agency. Use the following worksheet to list your licenses and certificates.

**CERTIFICATES AND LICENSES**

Name of License: _____

Licensing Agency: _____

Date Issued: _____

Name of License: _____

Licensing Agency: _____

Date Issued: _____

Name of License: _____

Licensing Agency: _____

Date Issued: _____

## Professional Memberships

Another potential element in your resume is a section listing professional memberships. Use this section to list involvement in professional associations, unions, and similar organizations. It is to your advantage to list any professional memberships that pertain to the job you are seeking. Be sure to include the dates of your involvement and whether you took part in any special activities or held any offices within the organization. Use the following worksheet to gather your information.

**PROFESSIONAL MEMBERSHIPS**

Name of Organization: _____

Offices Held: _____

Activities: _____

Date(s): _____

Name of Organization: _____

Offices Held: _____

Activities: _____

Date(s): _____

Name of Organization: _____

Offices Held: _____

Activities: _____

Date(s): _____

Name of Organization: _____

Offices Held: _____

Activities: _____

Date(s): _____

# Special Skills

This section of your resume is set aside for mentioning any special abilities you have that could relate to the job you are seeking. This is the part of your resume where you have the opportunity to demonstrate certain talents and experiences that are not necessarily a part of your educational or work experience. Common examples include fluency in a foreign language, or knowledge of a particular computer application.

Special skills can encompass a wide range of your talents—remember to be sure that whatever skills you list relate to the type of work you are looking for.

## Personal Information

Some people include "Personal" information on their resumes. This is not generally recommended, but you might wish to include it if you think that something in your personal life, such as a hobby or talent, has some bearing on the position you are seeking. This type of information is often referred to at the beginning of an interview, when it is used as an "ice breaker." Of course, personal information regarding age, marital status, race, religion, or sexual preference should never appear on any resume.

## References

References are not usually listed on the resume, but a prospective employer needs to know that you have references who may be contacted if necessary. All that is necessary to include in your resume regarding references is a sentence at the bottom stating, "References are available upon request." If a prospective employer requests a list of references, be sure to have one ready. Also, check with whomever you list to see if it is all right for you to use them as a reference. Forewarn them that they may receive a call regarding a reference for you. This way they can be prepared to give you the best reference possible.

# Chapter Two

# WRITING YOUR RESUME

*N*ow that you have gathered together all of the information for each of the sections of your resume, it's time to write out each section in a way that will get the attention of whoever is reviewing it. The type of language you use in your resume will affect its success. You want to take the information you have gathered and translate it into a language that will cause a potential employer to sit up and take notice.

Resume writing is not like expository writing or creative writing. It embodies a functional, direct writing style and focuses on the use of action words. By using action words in your writing, you more effectively stress past accomplishments. Action words help demonstrate your initiative and highlight your talents. Always use verbs that show strength and reflect the qualities of a "doer." By using action words, you characterize yourself as a person who takes action, and this will impress potential employers.

The following is a list of verbs commonly used in resume writing. Use this list to choose the action words that can help your resume become a strong one:

| | |
|---|---|
| administered | introduced |
| advised | invented |
| analyzed | maintained |
| arranged | managed |
| assembled | met with |
| assumed responsibility | motivated |
| billed | negotiated |
| built | operated |
| carried out | orchestrated |
| channeled | ordered |
| collected | organized |
| communicated | oversaw |
| compiled | performed |
| completed | planned |
| conducted | prepared |
| contacted | presented |
| contracted | produced |
| coordinated | programmed |
| counseled | published |
| created | purchased |
| cut | recommended |
| designed | recorded |
| determined | reduced |
| developed | referred |
| directed | represented |
| dispatched | researched |
| distributed | reviewed |
| documented | saved |
| edited | screened |
| established | served as |
| expanded | served on |
| functioned as | sold |
| gathered | suggested |
| handled | supervised |
| hired | taught |
| implemented | tested |
| improved | trained |
| inspected | typed |
| interviewed | wrote |

Now take a look at the information you put down on the work experience worksheets. Take that information and rewrite it in paragraph form, using verbs to highlight your actions and accomplishments. Let's look at an example, remembering that what matters here is the writing style, and not the particular job responsibilities given in our sample.

**WORK EXPERIENCE**
Regional Sales Manager

Manager of sales representatives from seven states. Responsible for twelve food chain accounts in the East. In charge of directing the sales force in planned selling toward specific goals. Supervisor and trainer of new sales representatives. Consulting for customers in the areas of inventory management and quality control.

*Special Projects*: Coordinator and sponsor of annual food industry sales seminar.

*Accomplishments*: Monthly regional volume went up 25 percent during my tenure while, at the same time, a proper sales/cost ratio was maintained. Customer/company relations improved significantly.

Below is the rewritten version of this information, using action words. Notice how much stronger it sounds.

**WORK EXPERIENCE**
Regional Sales Manager

Managed sales representatives from seven states. Handled twelve food chain accounts in the eastern United States. Directed the sales force in planned selling towards specific goals. Supervised and trained new sales representatives. Consulted for customers in the areas of inventory management and quality control. Coordinated and sponsored the annual Food Industry Seminar. Increased monthly regional volume 25 percent and helped to improve customer/company relations during my tenure.

Another way of constructing the work experience section is by using actual job descriptions. Job descriptions are rarely written using the proper resume language, but they do include all the information necessary to create this section of your resume. Take the description of one of the jobs your are including on your resume (if you have access to it), and turn it into an action-oriented paragraph. Below is an example of a job description followed by a version of the same description written using action words. Again, pay attention to the style of writing, as the details of your own work experience will be unique.

## PUBLIC ADMINISTRATOR I

*Responsibilities*: Coordinate and direct public services to meet the needs of the nation, state, or community. Analyze problems; work with special committees and public agencies; recommend solutions to governing bodies.

*Aptitudes and Skills*: Ability to relate to and communicate with people; solve complex problems through analysis; plan, organize, and implement policies and programs. Knowledge of political systems; financial management; personnel administration; program evaluation; organizational theory.

## WORK EXPERIENCE
Public Administrator I

Wrote pamphlets and conducted discussion groups to inform citizens of legislative processes and consumer issues. Organized and supervised 25 interviewers. Trained interviewers in effective communication skills.

Now that you have learned how to word your resume, you are ready for the next step in your quest for a winning resume: assembly and layout.

# Chapter Three

# ASSEMBLY AND LAYOUT

*A*t this point, you've gathered all the necessary information for your resume, and you've rewritten it using the language necessary to impress potential employers. Your next step is to assemble these elements in a logical order and then to lay them out on the page neatly and attractively in order to achieve the desired effect: getting that interview.

## Assembly

The order of the elements in a resume makes a difference in its overall effect. Obviously, you would not want to put your name and address in the middle of the resume or your special skills section at the top. You want to put the elements in an order that stresses your most important achievements, not the less pertinent information. For example, if you recently graduated from school and have no full-time work experience, you will want to list your education before you list any part-time jobs you may have held during school. On the other hand, if you have been gainfully employed for several years and currently hold an important position in your company, you will want to list your work experience ahead of your education, which has become less pertinent with time.

There are some elements that are always included in your resume and some that are optional. Following is a list of essential and optional elements:

| *Essential* | *Optional* |
|---|---|
| Name | Job Objective |
| Address | Honors |
| Phone Number | Special Skills |
| Work Experience | Professional Memberships |
| Education | Activities |
| References Phrase | Certificates and Licenses |
| | Personal Information |

Your choice of optional sections depends on your own background and employment needs. Always use information that will put you and your abilities in a favorable light. If your honors are impressive, then be sure to include them in your resume. If your activities in school demonstrate particular talents necessary for the job you are seeking, then allow space for a section on activities. Each resume is unique, just as each person is unique.

# Types of Resumes

So far, our discussion about resumes has involved the most common type—the *reverse chronological* resume, in which your most recent job is listed first and so on. This is the type of resume usually preferred by human resources directors, and it is the one most frequently used. However, in some cases this style of presentation is not the most effective way to highlight your skills and accomplishments.

For someone reentering the work force after many years or someone looking to change career fields, the *functional resume* may work best. This type of resume focuses more on achievement and less on the sequence of your work history. In the functional resume, your experience is presented by what you have accomplished and the skills you have developed in your past work.

A functional resume can be assembled from the same information you collected for your chronological resume. The main difference lies in how you organize this information. Essentially, the work experience section becomes two sections, with your job duties and accomplishments comprising one section and your employer's name, city, state, your position, and the dates employed making up another section. The first section is placed near the top of the resume, just below the job objective section, and can be called *Accomplishments* or *Achievements*. The second section, containing the bare essentials of your employment history, should come after the accomplishments section and can be titled *Work Experience* or *Employment History*. The other sections of your resume remain the same. The work experience section is the only one affected in the functional resume. By placing the section that focuses on your achievements first, you thereby draw attention to these achievements. This puts less emphasis on who you worked for and more emphasis on what you did and what you are capable of doing.

For someone changing careers, emphasis on skills and achievements is essential. The identities of previous employers, which may be unrelated to one's new job field, need to be downplayed. The functional resume accomplishes this task. For someone reentering the work force after many years, a functional resume is the obvious choice. If you lack full-time work experience, you will need to draw attention away from this fact and instead focus on your skills and abilities gained possibly through volunteer activities or part-time work. Education may also play a more important role in this resume.

Which type of resume is right for you will depend on your own personal circumstances. It may be helpful to create a chronological *and* a functional resume and then compare the two to find out which is more suitable. The sample resumes found in this book include both chronological and functional resumes. Use these resumes as guides to help you decide on the content and appearance of your own resume.

## Layout

Once you have decided which elements to include in your resume and you have arranged them in an order that makes sense and emphasizes your achievements and abilities, then it is time to work on the physical layout of your resume.

There is no single appropriate layout that applies to every resume, but there are a few basic rules to follow in putting your resume on paper:

1. Leave a comfortable margin on the sides, top, and bottom of the page (usually 1 to 1 1/2 inches).

2. Use appropriate spacing between the sections (usually 2 to 3 line spaces are adequate).

3. Be consistent in the *type* of headings you use for the different sections of your resume. For example, if you capitalize the heading EMPLOYMENT HISTORY, don't use initial capitals and underlining for a heading of equal importance, such as Education.

4. Always try to fit your resume onto one page. If you are having trouble fitting all your information onto one page, perhaps you are trying to say too much. Try to edit out any repetitive or unnecessary information or possibly shorten descriptions of earlier jobs. Be ruthless. Maybe you've included too many optional sections.

## CHRONOLOGICAL RESUME

Franklin Wu
5391 Southward Plaza
Walnut Creek, CA  94596
(510) 555-9008

**JOB OBJECTIVE:**   To obtain a position as a high-level optician in a fast-paced retail store.

**EDUCATION:**   Graduated Hayward Community College, Hayward, CA in June of 1986.

Graduated North Central High School, Chicago, IL in June of 1984.

**WORK EXPERIENCE:**

1990 - present   Great Spectacles, Walnut Creek, CA
Management Optician

1988 - 1990   Valley Vision, Pleasanton, CA
Management Optician and Frame Buyer

1986 - 1988   Dublin Optometry, Dublin, CA
File Clerk

**SPECIAL QUALIFICATIONS:**   People person; fashion styling experience; knowledge of adjustments, repairs and fittings of glasses and contact lenses.

**CERTIFICATION:**   American Board of Optometry Certificate

**CLASSES AND SEMINARS:**   Cal-Q Optics to prepare for licensing, 1992
Opti-Fair - annual, three day seminars

**REFERENCES:**   George Jones, O.D.
Great Spectacles, (510) 555-8941

Maria Lazar, Optician
Valley Vision, (510) 555-3726

# FUNCTIONAL RESUME

RESUME OF QUALIFICATIONS
OF
PATRICIA WHITE

987 West 44th Street
Cheyenne, WY 82001
(307) 555-9872

## PROFESSIONAL OBJECTIVE

Opportunity to demonstrate superior managerial ability and administrative decision-making skills in a nursing home environment.

## SUMMARY OF QUALIFICATIONS

- Highly organized and motivated.

- Ability and patience to train and develop office and professional staff.

- Thorough knowledge of computers - IBM PC, Lotus 1-2-3, WordPerfect, Symphony Data Base, IBM 38, typing, 10-key by touch, dictaphone, and 2-way radio system.

- Extensive experience in all phases of geriatric care: management, accounting, and medical treatment.

- Good rapport with all levels of employees, patients and their families, and public agencies.

## EDUCATION

University of Wyoming, B.A. Business
Laramie, WY

## EXPERIENCE

1985-Present - Assistant Director, Longview Manor, Cheyenne, WY

1983-1985 - Business Manager, Mountain Top Nursing Home, Cheyenne, WY

## REFERENCES

Excellent professional and personal references

Don't let the idea of having to tell every detail about your life get in the way of producing a resume that is simple and straightforward. The more compact your resume, the easier it will be to read and the better an impression it will make for you.

In some cases, the resume will not fit on a single page, even after extensive editing. In such cases, the resume should be printed on two pages so as not to compromise clarity or appearance. Each page of a two-page resume should be marked clearly with your name and the page number, e.g., "Judith Ramirez, page 1 of 2." The pages should then be stapled together.

Try experimenting with various layouts until you find one that looks good to you. Always show your final layout to other people and ask them what they like or dislike about it, and what impresses them most about your resume. Make sure that is what you want most to emphasize. If it isn't, you may want to consider making changes in your layout until the necessary information is emphasized. Use the sample resumes in this book to get some ideas for laying out your resume.

## Putting Your Resume in Print

Your resume should be typed or printed on good quality 8½″ × 11″ bond paper. You want to make as good an impression as possible with your resume; therefore, quality paper is a necessity. If you have access to a word processor with a good printer, or know of someone who does, make use of it. Typewritten resumes should only be used when there are no other options available.

After you have produced a clean original, you will want to make duplicate copies of it. Usually a copy shop is your best bet for producing copies without smudges or streaks. Make sure you have the copy shop use quality bond paper for all copies of your resume. Ask for a sample copy before they run your entire order. After copies are made, check each copy for cleanliness and clarity.

Another more costly option is to have your resume typeset and printed by a printer. This will provide the most attractive resume of all. If you anticipate needing a lot of copies of your resume, the cost of having it typeset may be justified.

# Proofreading

After you have finished typing the master copy of your resume and before you go to have it copied or printed, you must thoroughly check it for typing and spelling errors. Have several people read it over just in case you may have missed an error. Misspelled words and typing mistakes will not make a good impression on a prospective employer, as they are a bad reflection on your writing ability and your attention to detail. With thorough and conscientious proofreading, these mistakes can be avoided.

The following are some rules of capitalization and punctuation that may come in handy when proofreading your resume:

*Rules of Capitalization*

- Capitalize proper nouns, such as names of schools, colleges, and universities, names of companies, and brand names of products.
- Capitalize major words in the names and titles of books, tests, and articles that appear in the body of your resume.
- Capitalize words in major section headings of your resume.
- Do not capitalize words just because they seem important.
- When in doubt, consult a manual of style such as *Words Into Type* (Prentice-Hall), or *The Chicago Manual of Style* (The University of Chicago Press). Your local library can help you locate these and other reference books.

*Rules of Punctuation*

- Use a comma to separate words in a series.
- Use a semicolon to separate series of words that already include commas within the series.
- Use a semicolon to separate independent clauses that are not joined by a conjunction.
- Use a period to end a sentence.
- Use a colon to show that the examples or details that follow expand or amplify the preceding phrase.
- Avoid the use of dashes.
- Avoid the use of brackets.
- If you use any punctuation in an unusual way in your resume, be consistent in its use.
- Whenever you are uncertain, consult a style manual.

# Chapter Four

# THE COVER LETTER

*O*nce your resume has been assembled, laid out, and printed to your satisfaction, the next and final step before distribution is to write your cover letter. Though there may be instances where you deliver your resume in person, most often you will be sending it through the mail. Resumes sent through the mail always need an accompanying letter that briefly introduces you and your resume. The purpose of the cover letter is to get a potential employer to read your resume, just as the purpose of your resume is to get that same potential employer to call you for an interview.

Like your resume, your cover letter should be clean, neat, and direct. A cover letter usually includes the following information:

1.  Your name and address (unless it already appears on your personal letterhead).

2.  The date.

3.  The name and address of the person and company to whom you are sending your resume.

4.  The salutation ("Dear Mr." or "Dear Ms." followed by the person's last name, or "To Whom It May Concern" if you are answering a blind ad).

5.  An opening paragraph explaining why you are writing (in response to an ad, the result of a previous meeting, at the suggestion of someone you both know) and indicating that you are interested in whatever job is being offered.

6. One or two more paragraphs that tell why you want to work for the company and what qualifications and experience you can bring to that company.

7. A final paragraph that closes the letter and requests that you be contacted for an interview. You may mention here that your references are available upon request.

8. The closing ("Sincerely," or "Yours Truly," followed by your signature with your name typed under it).

Your cover letter, including all of the information above, should be no more than one page in length. The language used should be polite, businesslike, and to the point. Do not attempt to tell your life story in the cover letter. A long and cluttered letter will only serve to put off the reader. Remember, you only need to mention a few of your accomplishments and skills in the cover letter. The rest of your information is in your resume. Each and every achievement should not be mentioned twice. If your cover letter is a success, your resume will be read and all pertinent information reviewed by your prospective employer.

## Producing the Cover Letter

Cover letters should always be typed individually, since they are always written to particular individuals and companies. Never use a form letter for your cover letter. Cover letters cannot be copied or reproduced like resumes. Each one should be as personal as possible. Of course, once you have written and rewritten your first cover letter to the point where you are satisfied with it, you certainly can use similar wording in subsequent letters.

After you have typed your cover letter on quality bond paper, be sure to proofread it as thoroughly as you did your resume. Again, spelling errors are a sure sign of carelessness, and you don't want that to be a part of your first impression on a prospective employer. Make sure to handle the letter and resume carefully to avoid any smudges, and then mail both your cover letter and resume in an appropriate sized envelope. Be sure to keep an accurate record of all the resumes you send out and the results of each mailing, either in a separate notebook or on individual $3 \times 5''$ index cards.

Numerous sample cover letters appear at the end of the book. Use them as models for your own cover letter or to get an idea of how cover letters are put together. Remember, every one is unique and depends on the particular circumstances of the individual writing it and the job for which he or she is applying.

# Chapter Five

# SAMPLE RESUMES

This chapter contains dozens of sample resumes for people pursuing a wide variety of jobs and careers within this field.

There are many different styles of resumes in terms of graphic layout and presentation of information. These samples also represent people with varying amounts of education and work experience. Use these samples to model your own resume after. Choose one resume, or borrow elements from several different resumes to help you construct your own.

CURRICULUM VITAE

HANNA MA, M.D.

**HOME ADDRESS**

111 Barclay
Cincinnati, OH 45219
Phone: 513/555-7987

**WORK ADDRESS**

Department of Nephrology
Henry Wilkins Hospital
2799 North Street
Cincinnati, OH 45219
Phone: 513/555-7659

**SPECIALTY**

Nephrology

**EDUCATION**

Undergraduate:

Notre Dame University
South Bend, IN
1973-1977
Degree: B.S., magna cum laude
Major: Accounting
Minors: Chemistry and biology

Graduate:

Indiana University
Bloomington, IN
1977-1978
Degree: M.B.A., magna cum laude
Concentration: Finance

Medical School:

Wayne State University
Dayton, OH
1983-1987
Degree: M.D.

Page 2 - Hanna Ma, M.D.

## TRAINING

Residency:
Department of Medicine
Memorial Hospital
Denver, CO
1987-1990
Program Director:  Robert Jackson, M.D.

650-bed tertiary care facility.  Worked in inpatient and ambulatory medicine including extensive ICU, CCU, Oncology, and Emergency Room medicine.  Performed multiple procedures:  central line placement, lumbar puncture, bone marrow biopsy, and ventilator management.

Current:
Fellow, Department of Nephrology & Hypertension
Henry Wilkins Hospital
Cincinnati, OH
1990-present
Program Director:  James Minor, M.D.

Clinical based program encompassing all phases of nephrology including hemodialysis, transplantation, CAPD and consultation. Upon completion, will have performed approximately 15 biopsies, 70 catheter accesses, and 156 peritoneal catheter placements.

## EXPERIENCE

General Motors Company, Casting Division
Dearborn, MI
Financial and Profit Analysis
6/81-7/83

General Motors Company, Casting Plant
Indianapolis, IN
Accounting and Financial Analysis
8/78-5/81

## CERTIFICATION

American Board of Internal Medicine Eligible, 1990 ACLS, BCLS - 1991

Page 3 - Hanna Ma, M.D.

PROFESSIONAL SOCIETIES

American Medical Association
American College of Physicians
American Society of Nephrology
National Kidney Foundation

PUBLICATIONS/RESEARCH

CAPD and Obesity
Metabolic Effects of Intraperitoneal Calcium Channel
   Blocker Usage in CAPD Patients

LICENSURE

State of Ohio, 1990
State of Colorado, 1989

REFERENCES

Furnished upon request.

**GRAHAM T. BOOKER**
2354 Fuller Place, Apt. 2C
Indianapolis, IN 46250
Residence: (317) 555-7896

Safety Instruction

Safety Management                                    Environmental Assessment

## EDUCATION

Bachelor of Science in Health and Safety Education, 1978
Indiana State University, Terre Haute, Indiana

### Relevant Courses

Personal health science                              Individual safety
Community health                                     Health biostatistics
Health & safety education                            Subjects in health
Epidemiology                                         Human ecology
Human anatomy                                        Health services

## EXPERIENCE

Indiana Army National Guard, 1985-present
Shelbyville, Indiana

**Company Executive Officer, 1987-1990**
Coordinated command service support requirements. Responsible for all logistics. Counseled and performed annual evaluations for personnel as well as solicited suggestions for procedural improvements. Conducted all physical fitness training.

- Appointed company safety officer, planned and conducted safety classes.

- Representative to Indiana Army National Guard Safety Council.

- Appointed Unit Marshal, enforced military justice at the company level.

**Indiana State University Department of Recreation, 1985-1987**
**Terre Haute, Indiana**

**Lifeguard**
Oversaw the safety of all individuals in the pool area.  Improved and implemented safety procedures. Trained new lifeguards.

- Completed cardiopulmonary resuscitation and emergency first aid course.

**AGA Fleet Products, 1978-1985**
**Indianapolis, Indiana**

**Distribution services clerk.**

### MILITARY SERVICE

- Completed Army Helicopter Flight School Training November, 1990.

- Serve as 1st Lieutenant in the Indiana Army National Guard.

- Received Air Crewman's Badge, Army Service Ribbon, Army Commendation Medal, Army Aviator Badge.

- Completed Officer Candidate School while a full-time college student.

## Curriculum Vitae

Omar J. Jaksas

| | |
|---|---|
| **Education:** | -St. Edward's University, Austin, TX, 6/79-12/79<br>-Austin Community College, Austin, TX, 8/79-5/80<br>-Texas University at Austin, 6/80-6/82; Degree: B.S. in Biology<br>-FICTC Medical School, Santa Anna, D.R., 8/82-12/82<br>-URWAR Medical School, Santa Anna, D.R., 1/83-9/85; Degree: M.D. |
| **Postgraduate Training:** | -Frankford Hospital, Tory, PA, 7/86-6/87, Transitional Internship<br>-Presbyterian-University of PA, Tory, PA, 7/87-6/90, Internal Medicine Residency<br>-Mt. Sinai Medical Center, New York, NY, 7/90-present, Nephrology Fellowship |
| **Examinations & Licensures:** | -FMGMS passed in 7/85 (ECFMG License #555555555)<br>-FLEX passed in 6/86<br>-Internal Medicine Board passed in 9/90<br>-DEA License #BK-55555<br>-PA State License #MD-55555-L in 4/88<br>-NY State License #555555 in 4/90<br>-Internal Medicine License #555555 |
| **Awards:** | -B.S. in Biology with Honors<br>-M.D. with All Honors |
| **Memberships:** | -Alpha Epsilon Delta<br>-American College of Physicians<br>-American Medical Association<br>-Renal Physicians Association<br>-The National Kidney Foundation |
| **Background:** | -Volunteer Rescue Worker in Lebanon, 1976-78<br>-Volunteer Nurses' Aid in Austin, 1980<br>-Volunteer Physician Assistant in Austin, 10/85-4/86<br>-Fluent in English, Spanish, French, and Arabic |

## CURRICULUM VITAE

**NAME**                              THOMAS K. BODLE

**ADDRESS**                           APT 555, 555 STILL DR.
                                      SASKATOON, SASKATCHEWAN
                                      CANADA   S7J 4M7

**PHONE**                             HOSP (232) 555-4554
                                      WORK (343) 555-7680

**EXAMINATIONS PASSED**

1.   FMGEMS PART I - JANUARY 1988.

2.   MEDICAL COUNCIL OF CANADA EVALUATION EXAM - MARCH 1989.

3.   FMGEMS PART II - MAY 1989.

4.   MEDICAL COUNCIL OF CANADA QUALIFYING EXAM (LMCC) - MAY 1990.

5.   FLEX EXAMINATION - JUNE 1990.

6.   FRCP (INTERNAL MEDICINE, WRITTEN COMPONENT) - MAY 1991.

**CURRENT POSITION**

RESIDENT IV IN INTERNAL MEDICINE AT THE DEPARTMENT OF MEDICINE, THE
QUEENS HOSPITAL, SASKATOON, SASK, CANADA, S7N YYY.
JULY 1991-PRESENT.

**EXAMINATION TAKEN AND RESULTS AWAITED**

AMERICAN BOARD OF INTERNAL MEDICINE:  24 AND 25, SEPTEMBER 1991.

**ACADEMIC QUALIFICATIONS**

M.B.B.S. (UNDERGRADUATE            JANUARY 1977
MEDICAL DEGREE)                    INDIANA UNIVERSITY
                                   INDIANAPOLIS, IN

| | |
|---|---|
| M.D. (INTERNAL MEDICINE) (POSTGRADUATE SPECIALTY) | SEPTEMBER 1981 INDIANA UNIVERSITY INDIANAPOLIS, IN |
| DIPLOMATE OF NATIONAL BOARD (NEPHROLOGY) (SUBSPECIALTY DEGREE) | NOVEMBER 1984 NATIONAL BOARD OF MEDICAL EXAMINATIONS INDIANA MEDICAL CENTER |

**DETAILS OF TRAINING AND POSITIONS HELD IN CHRONOLOGICAL ORDER AFTER GRADUATION IN 1977**

MARCH 1977 – FEB 1978     COMPULSORY ROTATION INTERNSHIP IN COMBINED HOSPITALS ATTACHED TO INDIANA MEDICAL COLLEGE. ROTATIONS INCLUDED MEDICINE, SURGERY, OBSTETRICS AND GYNECOLOGY, COMMUNITY MEDICINE AND PUBLIC HEALTH, ORTHOPAEDICS, PSYCHIATRY, OTORHINOLARYNGOLOGY, OPHTHALMOLOGY, DERMATOLOGY, AND EMERGENCY MEDICINE. INDIANAPOLIS, IN.

MARCH 1978 – MAY 1978     FAMILY PRACTICE, TROY, PA.

JUNE 1978 – AUG 1978     SENIOR HOUSE OFFICER IN INTERNAL MEDICINE IN THE DEPARTMENT OF MEDICINE, TROY MEDICAL COLLEGE, TROY, PA.

SEPT 1978 – AUG 1981     THREE YEARS OF CORE TRAINING AS RESIDENT IN MEDICINE AT THE DEPARTMENT OF INTERNAL MEDICINE, VICTORIA HOSPITAL, BANGOR, ME.

JAN 1982 – JAN 1984     TWO YEARS OF SUBSPECIALTY TRAINING AS A FELLOW IN NEPHROLOGY IN THE DEPARTMENT OF NEPHROLOGY AT CHRISTIAN MEDICAL COLLEGE AND HOSPITAL, BOSTON, MA.

FEB 1984 – NOV 1984     SENIOR REGISTRAR IN NEPHROLOGY, DEPARTMENT OF NEPHROLOGY AT CHRISTIAN MEDICAL COLLEGE AND HOSPITAL, BOSTON, MA.

NOV 1984 – JULY 1985     LECTURER IN NEPHROLOGY, DEPARTMENT OF NEPHROLOGY, CHRISTIAN MEDICAL COLLEGE AND HOSPITAL, BOSTON, MA.

AUG 1985 – JUNE 1987     ASSISTANT PROFESSOR IN MEDICINE, DEPARTMENT OF MEDICINE AT ST. MARY'S COLLEGE AND HOSPITAL, LAFAYETTE, IN.

JULY 1987 - JUNE 1989     TWO YEARS OF FELLOWSHIP TRAINING IN NEPHROLOGY IN THE DIVISION OF NEPHROLOGY, DEPARTMENT OF INTERNAL MEDICINE AT THE UNIVERSITY OF QUEENS HOSPITAL, ALBERTA, CANADA.

JULY 1989 - JUNE 1991     THREE YEARS OF CORE TRAINING IN INTERNAL MEDICINE, DEPARTMENT OF MEDICINE, UNIVERSITY OF QUEENS HOSPITAL, ALBERTA, CANADA.

## AWARDS AND SCHOLARSHIPS

RESIDENT RESEARCH PROJECT TOP PRIZE FOR THE YEAR 1990-91: CYCLOSPORIN AND DISTAL RENAL TUBULAR DYSFUNCTION IN RENAL TRANSPLANT PATIENTS, DEPARTMENT OF MEDICINE, UNIVERSITY OF QUEENS HOSPITAL, ALBERTA, CANADA.

SOCIAL AND EDUCATIONAL SCHOLARSHIP OF THE PROVINCIAL GOVERNMENT DURING UNDERGRADUATE MEDICAL COURSE AWARDED FOR 5 YEARS FROM 1972-76, INDIANA UNIVERSITY.

## ADMINISTRATIVE POSTS

1.  ADMINISTRATIVE RESIDENT, DEPARTMENT OF MEDICINE, AT THE VALLEY HEALTH CENTER, ALBERTA, FOR THE YEAR 1990.

2.  ORGANIZING SECRETARY, 6TH ANNUAL CONFERENCE OF SOUTHERN CHAPTER OF NEPHROLOGY, OCTOBER 1986.

3.  COORDINATOR, SCIENTIFIC SESSION 15TH ANNUAL CONFERENCE OF NEPHROLOGY, 1985.

## PROFESSIONAL EXPERIENCE

1.  INVESTIGATION, DIAGNOSIS, AND MANAGEMENT OF ALL VARIETIES OF CLINICAL NEPHROLOGY PROBLEMS.

2.  HEMODIALYSIS (INSERTION OF SUBCLAVIAN, JUGULAR, FEMORAL LINES; CREATION OF SCRIBNER SHUNTS; MONITORING; AND FOLLOW-UP OF ACUTE AND CHRONIC HEMODIALYSIS PATIENTS).

3.  PERITONEAL DIALYSIS (INSERTION OF ACUTE PERITONEAL DIALYSIS, MONITORING, AND FOLLOW-UP OF PATIENTS ON ACUTE AND CHRONIC PERITONEAL DIALYSIS).

## PROFESSIONAL EXPERIENCE (CONT.)

4.  RENAL BIOPSIES (300 ADULT BIOPSIES, 75 TRANSPLANT BIOPSIES, AND 30 PEDIATRIC BIOPSIES).

5.  LIVE DONOR KIDNEY PERFUSION (150 KIDNEY PERFUSIONS).

6.  RENAL TRANSPLANT RECIPIENT MONITORING AND POST TRANSPLANT FOLLOW-UP INCLUDING EVALUATION OF COMPLICATIONS, MANAGEMENT OF REJECTION EPISODES, ETC. (EXPERIENCE OF ABOUT 300 RENAL TRANSPLANTS).

7.  RENAL CONSULTATIONS.

## TEACHING EXPERIENCE

1.  THEORY CLASSES IN INTERNAL MEDICINE AND NEPHROLOGY FOR UNDERGRADUATE STUDENTS.

2.  BEDSIDE CLINICAL TEACHING FOR UNDERGRADUATE AND POSTGRADUATE STUDENTS IN INTERNAL MEDICINE.

3.  SEMINARS, GRAND ROUNDS, TEACHING ROUNDS, JOURNAL CLUB MEETINGS.

4.  CLASSES FOR M.S. (NURSING COURSE) IN MEDICINE.

5.  CLASSES FOR DIALYSIS DIPLOMA STUDENTS.

## RESEARCH EXPERIENCE

I HAVE BEEN INTERESTED IN TRANSPLANT IMMUNOLOGY RESEARCH AND HAVE DONE ONE YEAR OF BENCH RESEARCH IN STUDYING THE SIGNIFICANCE OF ANTI HLA CLASS I ANTIBODIES IN RENAL TRANSPLANT RECIPIENTS AND THEIR ROLE IN THE CAUSATION OF REJECTION EPISODES. THIS WORK WAS SUPPORTED BY A GRANT FROM THE ALBERTA HERITAGE FUND AND WAS PRESENTED AT THE AMERICAN TRANSPLANT SOCIETY ANNUAL MEETING, HELD IN CHICAGO IN 1989, AND THE AMERICAN SOCIETY OF NEPHROLOGY MEETING, HELD IN AUSTIN IN 1988.

## MISCELLANEOUS

1.  RESPONSIBLE FOR SETTING UP DIALYSIS AND TRANSPLANT UNIT AT M.S. QUEENS MEDICAL COLLEGE AND HOSPITAL, APRIL, 1987.

2.  MEMBER, ASSOCIATION OF PHYSICIANS OF AMERICA.

3.  MEMBER, SOUTHERN CHAPTER SOCIETY OF NEPHROLOGY.

4.  MEMBER, CANADA MEDICAL ASSOCIATION.

**ANNETTE P. KEITH**
555 Viewmall Drive, Apt.#2
Yonkers, NY 10710
(914) 555-6892

## PROFESSIONAL EXPERIENCE

| | |
|---|---|
| July 89-June 91 | Fellowship in Nephrology at Albert College of Medicine, Bronx, New York. |
| July 86-June 89 | Residency in Internal Medicine at New York Hospital, Queens, New York, affiliated to New York Hospital, Cornell University, Ithaca, New York. |
| May 82-Oct 84 | Medical Officer, Brazil, South America. |
| Oct 80-April 81 | Postgraduate resident at Kayo Medical College Hospital, Kayo, Mexico. |
| April 79-April 80 | Rotating Internship at the Queens Hospital, Queens Medical College, Queens University, Bronx, New York. |

## CERTIFYING EXAMINATIONS

| | |
|---|---|
| June 91 | Eligible to appear for The American Board of Nephrology Examination. |
| Sept 89 | Diplomate of The American Board of Internal Medicine. |
| Dec 86 | FLEX, New York State. (83% and 86%) |
| Jan 85 | FMGEMS. (85%) |

## EDUCATION

| | |
|---|---|
| Sept 74-Aug 80 | Bachelor of Medicine and Bachelor of Surgery (M.B.B.S.), Queens Medical College, Bronx, New York. |
| June 72-Mar 74 | Pre-Medical Course at The National College, Queens University, Bronx, New York. |

## LICENSES

| | |
|---|---|
| July 89 | New York State, No: 555555. |
| May 80 | Mexico, No: 5555. |

## AWARDS AND HONORS

**Medical**                         Class of 110 students.
                                    12th rank in final M.B.B.S. Exam.
                                    1st rank in second M.B.B.S. Exam.
                                    1st rank in first M.B.B.S. Exam.

**Pre-Medical**                     State level examination.
                                    11th rank in second year.
                                    4th rank in first year.

## MEMBERSHIPS

1.   Member of the American College of Physicians.

## REFERENCES

1.   Dr. Sara Joseph, M.D., Chief, Division of Nephrology, Queens Medical College, Bronx, New York.
     (212) 555-8927.

2.   Dr. Jason Wilcox, M.D., Chief, Division of Nephrology, Memorial Medical Center, Bronx, New York.
     (212) 555-6890.

3.   Dr. Kerry Piller, M.D., Chief, Department of Medicine, St. Joseph Medical Center, Bronx, New York.
     (212) 555-9900.

4.   Dr. Meredith Hulecki, M.D., Associate Professor of Medicine, Memorial Medical Center, Bronx, New
     York.  (212) 555-0000.

## CURRICULUM VITAE

**Richard A. Langner, M.D.**
**5555 N. Senate Ave., Suite 555**
**Indianapolis, Indiana 46202**

**PERSONAL DATA**

| | |
|---|---|
| **Residence Address:** | **1111 N. Illinois**<br>**Indianapolis, IN 46208** |
| **Telephone:** | **(317) 555-3333** |
| **Military Service:** | **United States Navy**<br>**Rank: Commander**<br>**June 1970-July 1981** |

**EDUCATION AND TRAINING**

| | |
|---|---|
| **Pre-Medical Education:** | **Notre Dame University**<br>**South Bend, Indiana**<br>**B.A. Degree**<br>**1962-1966** |
| **Medical School:** | **Indiana University**<br>**Indianapolis, Indiana**<br>**M.D. Degree**<br>**1967-1970** |
| **Internship:** | **National Naval Medical Center**<br>**Bethesda, Maryland**<br>**Surgical Internship**<br>**1970-1971** |
| **Residency:** | **Naval Regional Medical Center**<br>**Portsmouth, Virginia**<br>**General Surgery**<br>**1971-1975** |
| | **National Naval Medical Center**<br>**Bethesda, Maryland**<br>**Plastic Surgery**<br>**1975-1977** |

Richard A. Langner, M.D.
Page 2

| | |
|---|---|
| **Board Certification:** | **American Board of Plastic and Reconstructive Surgery, 1985** |

## TEACHING APPOINTMENTS

| | |
|---|---|
| **1977-1981:** | **Assistant Clinical Professor**<br>**Naval Regional Medical Center** |

## SPECIAL TRAINING

| | |
|---|---|
| **October 1983:** | **University of California**<br>**San Diego, California**<br>**Microvascular Surgery Techniques** |
| **March 1984:** | **Memorial Medical Center**<br>**Long Beach, California**<br>**Hyperbaric Oxygen Therapy** |
| **May 1988:** | **Midwestern Regional Lipoplasty Symposium**<br>**Minneapolis, Minnesota**<br>**Liposuction** |

## MEMBERSHIPS

| | |
|---|---|
| **International Microsurgical Society** | **American Medical Association** |
| **American Burn Association** | **Diplomate American Board of**<br>**Plastic Surgery** |
| **American Association of Tissue**<br>**Banks** | |

## DIRECTORSHIPS/CHAIRMANSHIPS

| | |
|---|---|
| **Consultant**<br>**Hyperbaric Oxygen Therapy**<br>**Memorial Hospital**<br>**1985-Present** | **Chairman**<br>**Decubitus Ulcer Task Force**<br>**Memorial Hospital**<br>**1989-Present** |
| **Consultant**<br>**Tissue Bank**<br>**Central Indiana Blood Ctr.**<br>**1987-1988** | **Director of Wound Care Task**<br>**Force**<br>**Memorial Hospital**<br>**1989-Present** |
| **Burn Director**<br>**Memorial Hospital**<br>**1988-Present** | **Director of Hyperbaric**<br>**Oxygen Medicine**<br>**Humana Womens Hospital**<br>**1990-Present** |

**Richard A. Langner, M.D.**
**Page 3**

**PUBLICATIONS**

**Malignant Hyperthermia During Repair of a Cleft Lip, L.P. Gisler, D. Wroblewski, R.A. Langner, ANNALS OF PLASTIC SURGERY, Vol. 2, No.5, pp. 550-562.**

**PRESENTATIONS**

| | |
|---|---|
| **May 1988:** | **CLINITRON BENEFITS - Guest speaker at Support Systems International St. Petersburg, Florida** |
| **October 1990:** | **TECHNIQUES OF WOUND REPAIR - Guest speaker at 8th Annual Emergency Medicine Update Meeting Community Hospital of Indianapolis** |

**MEETINGS ATTENDED**

| | |
|---|---|
| **January 1980:** | **Symposia of Military Plastic Surgery Washington, D.C.** |
| **October 1980:** | **American Society of Plastic and Reconstructive Surgery New Orleans, Louisiana** |
| **October 1981:** | **American Association of Hand Surgery New York, New York** |
| **April 1982:** | **American Burn Association Meeting Cincinnati, Ohio** |
| **May 1983:** | **American Cleft Palate Association Indianapolis, Indiana** |
| **March 1985:** | **Plastic Surgery Education Foundation Meeting Steamboat Springs, Colorado** |
| **May 1988:** | **The Midwestern Regional Lipoplasty Symposium Indianapolis, Indiana** |
| **March 1989:** | **Midwest Regional Burn Meeting Cincinnati, Ohio** |
| **March 1990:** | **American Burn Association Meeting Las Vegas, Nevada** |

Darren C. Hanover
405 D Lane, Apt. 3C
Indianapolis, IN  46237

Telephone: (317) 555-8907
Work:      (317) 555-0987


EMPLOYER ADDRESS:

Pediatric Clinic
Hawley Community Hospital
Fort Wayne, IN  46216

POSITION SOUGHT:

Pediatric Nurse Practitioner

EDUCATION:

Formal:     Graduate:

Indiana University School of Nursing (IUPUI)
Health Maintenance of the Child
Indianapolis, IN
Master of Science in Nursing, 1985

            Undergraduate:

Medical College of Georgia
Augusta, GA
Bachelor of Science in Nursing, 1977

            Basic Nursing:

Auburn Memorial Hospital School of Nursing
Auburn, NY
Diploma in Nursing, 1971

            Other:

University of South Carolina
Columbia, SC
Associate Degree General Study, 1976

Auburn Community College
Auburn, NY
Affiliation with Basic Nursing School
Taking sciences appropriate to nursing

            Pediatric Nurse
            Practitioner:

Madigan Medical Center
Tacoma, WA
Certificate as Pediatric Nurse
Practitioner, 1972

Indiana University School of Nursing
Pediatric Nurse Associate Program as part of
graduate study

Pediatric Emergency Nursing Department of
Postgraduate Medicine & Health Professional
Education
The University of Michigan Medical School, Ann
Arbor, MI, 1985

7th Annual Nursing Conference on Pediatric
Primary Care, National Association of Pediatric
Nurse Associates and Practitioners, The PNP in
the Changing Health Care System, San Diego, CA,
1986

Further listings available upon request

**PROFESSIONAL
CREDENTIALS:**

RN License:      Indiana:  #55555555  Exp. 10/31/87
              New York:  #5555555  Exp. 10/31/86

Pediatric Nurse
Practitioner:      Certificate Madigan Medical Center, 1972

              The National Board of Pediatric Nurse Practitioners and Associates Certification, 1977 as Pediatric Nurse Practitioner ID #5555555

**PROFESSIONAL EXPERIENCE:**

Pediatric Nurse
Practitioner
Feb 1983
to present:      Hawley Community Hospital
              Pediatric Clinic
              Fort Wayne, IN  46216

              Duties:     Primary Care nurse in the Pediatric and Well Baby Clinic. Plan and develop methods, practices, and approaches pertinent to health maintenance of pediatric patients (birth to 18 years) and their families. The work covers a complete range of pediatric health services including assessment of patients, evaluating the effectiveness of care, initiating, changing or modifying treatment. This involves counseling, teaching, coordination of services, participating with other disciplines, development of new techniques, the establishment and revision of criteria for care. Also, act as clinical instructor and preceptor for graduate PNP students, RN students, and medical screening students planning and executing in-services. Responsible as Pediatric Nursing Consultant for the hospital, planning and executing parenting classes, and serving as a member of the Community Health Education Committee.

Pediatric Nurse
Practitioner
July 1980 to
Feb 1983:      Ireland Community Hospital
              Louisville, KY

              Duties:     Same as at Fort Wayne. In addition, responsible for all admission and discharge physicals on normal newborns including ordering, required studies and management of specific abnormalities. Gave all newborn pre- and postnatal classes.

                               Rotated as weekend hospital Nursing Supervisor. Served on the Audit and Community Health Education Committee.

Clinical Head
Nurse
July 1977 to
July 1980:        Tripler Medical Center
Honolulu, HI

        Duties:      In charge of a 33-bed pediatric medical-surgical ward caring for children requiring minimal to intensive care. Responsible for the administration and management of nursing activities on a busy pediatric ward through maximum utilization, evaluation, education, and training of nursing personnel. Supervised and was responsible for 10-12 RN's and 15-20 paraprofessionals and gave care to pediatric patients. As a Clinical Head Nurse, responsible for assessing, planning, directing, giving, and evaluating nursing care. Served as Hospital Nursing Supervisor 1-2 weekends per month and as Maternal and Child Supervisor when supervisor not present.

Pediatric Nurse
Practitioner,
Clinical Staff
and Head Nurse
Jan 1983 to
Aug 1976:      Moncrief Community Hospital
Charlotte, SC

        Duties:      First 4 months worked as staff nurse for all shifts in the nursery and pediatric ward, ending as Clinical Head Nurse. Responsible for introducing the role of the PNP to the Pediatric Clinic.

Clinical Staff
Nurse
Feb 1972 to
Dec 1972:      Madigan Medical Center
Tacoma, WA

        Duties:      Worked as a beginning level staff nurse in charge of evening shift. This involved care and supervision of care for medical-surgical pediatric patients up to age 18 years requiring minimal to intensive care. Supervised RN's and paraprofessionals during that shift.

PERSONAL DATA:      Birthdate  March 29, 1949
Married
Daughters - ages 10, 8, and 5 years

PROFESSIONAL ORGANIZATIONS:

1973 to Present: National Association of Pediatric Nurse Associates and Practitioners (became fellow in 1977).
1984 to Present: National Association of Pediatric Nurse Associates and Practitioners, Indiana Chapter.

References:      Available upon request or during interview.

## ANDREW JOHN BEAMS

Local Address
786 Zelda Street
Indianapolis, IN  46831
(317) 555-2299

Home Address
404 W. l6th St.
South Bend, IN 46628
(219) 555-4536

**OBJECTIVE:** To obtain employment in an environment where I can apply my knowledge of education and exercise my analytical and interpersonal skills.

**EDUCATION:** Temple University, Bachelor of Science with Honors in Education
Graduated in May, 1991          G.P.A.: 3.3/4.0

**EXPERIENCE:**

June 1991-
Present:

**Tri-West Services for Mental Health**
South Bend, Indiana
**Educational Attendant:** Involved in one-to-one contact with patients on the unit, including direct conversations, taking vital signs, recreational activities, and completing rounds.  Responsible for "charting" on individual patients and providing assessments of patients' physical and mental status.

June 1991-
Present:

**Valley, Inc.**
Indianapolis, Indiana
**Reformat Editor:** Member of a four-person effort to reformat "Valley's All Lines Service" (covering insurance agent/agency licensing) from a word processing format into a data base format.

**Temple University** (work/study program)
Philadelphia, Pennsylvania

Aug 1989-
May 1991:

**Computer Lab Assistant:** Assisted students with Macintosh usage.

Aug 1989-
May 1991:

**Faculty Assistant:** Worked in the education department doing odd jobs and clerical work for the professors.

Jan 1990-
Present:

**Research Assistant:** Assisted in scoring, coding, analyzing, and interpretation of data in various research areas.

May 1990-
Aug 1990:
        **Harrold's Nursery and Landscaping**
        Wabash, Indiana
        **Landscaper:** Completed various residential and commercial landscaping projects working together with a three or four man team.

**SPECIAL SKILLS:** I have worked with Macintosh computers and Microsoft Word extensively, and I am familiar with Delta Graph, Hypercard, and Excel. Also, I have had experience with two statistical packages, SuperANOVA and SPSSx, and I become acquainted with new software packages quickly.

**ACTIVITIES:** Member of the Phi Delta Theta Fraternity
        *Alumni secretary, Fall 1989
        *Pledge committee member, Fall 1988
        *Intramural softball
Member of the Education Club, Spring 1990-Present
Peer Academic Advisor, Fall 1990
Member of the Trinity Lutheran Church
Enjoy cycling and creative writing (short fiction)

KEVIN E. CODY
5555 Field Avenue
Fort Wayne, IN  46236
(219) 555-8976

OBJECTIVE

Staff nurse anesthetist position with room for supervisory advancement within two years in a modern, well-equipped, mid-sized, medical facility where CRNAs and MDAs support each other while retaining their own autonomy.

SUMMARY OF QUALIFICATIONS

Eleven years of clinical experience in small and large medical center settings, combining decision making with professional latitude.  Experienced in all types of general and regional anesthesia with continuous epidural experience in postoperative pain relief.  Possess strong interpersonal communication skills resulting in high degrees of patient satisfaction.

EXPERIENCE

1990 to present

Staff Anesthetist and Chief Anesthetist, Nurse Anesthesia Section.
Hawley Community Hospital, Fort Wayne, IN.

* Supervise and assume overall clinical and administrative responsibility for a two anesthetist operating setting averaging over 500 cases per year without the benefit of an assigned staff anesthesiologist.
* Serve as Technical Director and Quality Assurance Coordinator for Respiratory Therapy Services.  Perform duties of Chief, Department of Nursing, in her absence.
* Administer clinical anesthesia with call coverage, and provide continuous epidural postoperative pain management.

1987 to 1990

Staff Anesthetist and Assistant Supervisor, Nurse Anesthesia Section.
Brooke Medical Center, Houston, TX.

* Provided relief supervision and assistance to CRNA staff and anesthesia residents administering anesthesia on complex surgical procedures.
* Assisted with anesthesia supplies and new equipment ordering, maintenance, and evaluation.
* Served as Basic Cardiac Life Support (BCLS) Instructor for the anesthesia staff.
* Administered clinical anesthesia in medical center and Level I trauma center setting.

**1984 to 1987**

Chief and Assistant Chief, Nurse Anesthesia Section.
Moncrief Community Hospital, Charlotte, SC.

* Supervised staff of four CRNAs in operative setting averaging over 200 surgical cases per month.
* Managed anesthesia supply system resulting in successful compliance with projected budgetary constraints.
* Converted daily anesthesia supply system to a daily cart exchange system to reduce time spent on daily restock.
* Administered clinical anesthesia with call coverage.

**1983 to 1984**

Staff Anesthetist and Clinical Instructor, Nurse Anesthesia Section.
Community Hospital, Richmond, VA.

* Provided clinical supervision of Community Hospital, Phase II nurse anesthesia students.
* Designed a departmental continuing education program with approved credit by the American Association of Nurse Anesthetists (AANA).
* Developed a departmental Quality Assurance Program.
* Administered clinical anesthesia with call coverage.

**1980 to 1983**

Staff Anesthetist, Nurse Anesthesia Section.
Memorial Hospital, Tulsa, OK.

* Developed departmental Quality Assurance Program.
* Developed departmental continuing education program with approved credit by the AANA.
* Developed a standardized anesthesia equipment set-up for hospital-wide use in all CPR carts.
* Evaluated and gained approval for purchase of a new anesthesia gas mass spectrometry monitoring system.
* Administered clinical anesthesia with call coverage.

EDUCATION

1990    Webster University, Master of Arts in Health Services Management.
1984    Baylor University, Bachelor of Science in Nursing.
1980    Academy of Health Sciences, Diploma in Nurse Anesthesia.

## AFFILIATIONS

American Association of Nurse Anesthetists.

## LICENSURE

Board of Nurse Examiners for the State of Texas No. 55555555.
Indiana State Board of Nursing No. 5555 (Temporary Permit).

## CERTIFICATION

Council on Recertification of Nurse Anesthetists No. 555555.

CURRICULUM VITAE

Michael Martinez

1.  PERSONAL DATA

    Interests:      Cycling, Camping, Hunting, Fishing,
                    Woodworking, Sports, Playing Guitar, Medical
                    Illustrating (see Section #7)

    Home:           455 Lilac Lane
                    Mooresville, IN  46158            317-555-7892

2.  EDUCATION

                                                 Degree     Date

    College:        Hanover College               B.A.     May 1988
                    Hanover, Indiana
                    Magna Cum Laude 3.93 GPA
                    Highest Departmental Honors
                    in Chemistry 4.00 GPA
                    First Team Academic All-American Football
                    Lineman - Co-Captain - Senior Year:  Four
                    Varsity Letters - National Football
                    Foundation and Hall of Fame Scholar
                    Athlete Award/Graduate Scholarship

    Medical
    School:         Indiana University            M.D.     May 1992
                    School of Medicine
                    Indianapolis, Indiana
                    Honors Marks:  Gross Anatomy, Systemic
                    Pathology, and Clerkships in Pediatrics and
                    Neuroscience.

3.  MILITARY EXPERIENCE

    Second Lieutenant Medical Officer Training               1989-91
    Corps - United States Army Reserve/Indiana
    National Guard

    Indiana Medical Advisory Committee Member                  1991

Michael Martinez                                                    -2-

4.    WORK EXPERIENCE

      Extern, Henry County Memorial Hospital               1990-91
      New Castle, Indiana

      Summer Research Intern, Methodist Sports Clinic         1990
      Donald C. Summers, M.D.
      Indianapolis, Indiana

5.    RESEARCH EXPERIENCE

      Senior Research Thesis in Department of Chemistry     1987-88
      Hanover College
      Robert M. Gibbons, PhD.
      Associate Professor of Chemistry
      Hanover, Indiana

      Summer Research Intern                                  1989
      Andrew M. Sporn, M.D.
      St. Vincent's Sports Clinic
      Indianapolis, Indiana

6.    BIBLIOGRAPHY

      1.    Gibbons R.M. and M.J. Murray: Forward and Reverse Rate
            Constants in the Diel-Alder Reaction.  Senior
            Research Thesis File, Duggan Library, Hanover
            College, Hanover, Indiana, May 1988.

      2.    Sporn, A.M. Jones, M.J. Murray, and K.L. Jones:
            Isolated Fractures of the Tibial Eminence in
            Adults Associated with Anterior Laxity.  Submitted
            for Publication 1991.

7.    MEDICAL ILLUSTRATIONS

      1.    Kingsman, M.A.: Neurovascular Injuries in the Wrists
            and Hands of Athletes, *Clinics in Sports Medicine*,
            Vol. 9, No. 2, April 1990.

      2.    Michaels, J.B. and M.E. Tory:  Meniscal
                            Transplantation, Presentation, Duke
                            University School of Medicine, Durham,
                            North Carolina, Fall 1991.

## RESUME OF LESLIE P. CHANDLER

**NAME:**                Leslie P. Chandler

**PRESENT ADDRESS:**     4812 Burlington Drive, Indianapolis, IN 46033

**PHONE NUMBER:**        (317) 555-1052

**MILITARY:**            Retired, United States Marine Corps.
                         January 1965 to February 1971

**OCCUPATION:**          Certified Prosthetist, Manager

**EMPLOYER:**            Indianapolis Artificial Limb Corp.
                         May 1970 to Present
                         20 N. Meridian Street, Indianapolis, IN 46022
                         (317) 555-0987
                         (317) 555-8765

**PROSTHETIC EDUCATION:**

Northwestern University, School of Prosthetics - June 1972 to May
   1974, 1976, 1985
Chicago, Illinois

Courses Studied:    Below Knee Prosthetics for Prosthetists
                    Above Knee Prosthetics for Prosthetists
                    Upper Extremity Prosthetics for Prosthetists
                    Review Course in Prosthetics
                    1976:  Immediate Post-Surgical Fitting for
                       Prosthetists
                    1985:  Normal Shape, Normal Alignment Above
                       Knee Prosthesis

University of California, Los Angeles - UCLA Extension March 1987
Los Angeles, California

Course Studied:       Suction Below Knee Prosthetics

American Academy of Orthotics & Prosthetics - March 1973
St. Louis, Missouri

Course Studied:       Modular Prosthetic and Fluid Control
                      Mechanisms


**PROSTHETIC CERTIFICATION:**

American Board
  Certification:      October 9, 1974, Certificate as V.A.

Qualified
  Prosthetist:        May 15, 1975, #555


**CONTINUED EDUCATION COURSES PRESENTED BY VARIOUS MANUFACTURERS OF PROSTHETIC COMPONENTS AND SERVICE:**

April 1982:           Otto Bock Orthopedic Industry, Inc.
                      Minneapolis, Minnesota

                      Course:   Lower Extremity Modular System

February 1984:        Motion Control
                      Salt Lake City, Utah

                      Course:   Fitting Procedures of the Utah
                                Artificial Arm

April 1985:           Durr-Fillauer Medical, Inc.
                      Chattanooga, Tennessee

                      Course:   Scandinavian Flexible Socket

August 1985:          IPOS
                      Niagara Falls, New York

                      Course:   Flexible Socket Fabrication

May 1986:           Otto Bock Orthopedic Industry, Inc.
                         Minneapolis, Minnesota

                         Course:   Myoelectrically Controlled Upper
                                       Extremity System MYOBOCK

October 1987:       Flex-Foot, Inc.
                         Irving, California

                         Course:   Basic Flex-Foot

**CURRENT MEMBER OF THE FOLLOWING PROSTHETIC CLINICS FOR PATIENT MANAGEMENT, EVALUATION, AND PROSTHETIC CARE:**

1974 to Present:    Veterans Administration Medical Center

1985 to Present:    Ball Memorial Hospital, Muncie, Indiana

Alexander Clarke
85 Starview Lane
Kalamazoo, MI 49002
(616) 555-6812

## CAREER OBJECTIVE

A health care administrator in a hospital or clinic for the mildly mentally handicapped.

## EDUCATION

Bachelor of Science, December 1991
Major:  Psychology
Ball State University, Muncie, Indiana

Grades:               3.32/4.0 (major), 3.49/4.0 (overall)

Honors:               Kappa Delta Tau (Honor Society in Psychology)
                      Dean's List (5 times)

## PROFESSIONAL EXPERIENCE

1/92-4/92:            **Managing Director, Craig L. Turner Clinic,** Muncie, Indiana.
                     Responsible for operation of the clinic, which includes financial
                     planning, personnel, and cost control. Coordinated nursing and medical
                     activities.

## WORK EXPERIENCE

6/91-8/91:           **Assistant Director, Kelly Hospital,** Indianapolis, Indiana.  Managed
                     medical records department, inpatient admittance, and budget
                     planning.

4/91-5/91:           **Administrative Supervisor, Muncie Community Hospitals,** Muncie,
                     Indiana.  Trained personnel, hired staff, and administered educational
                     services.

8/88-12/90:          **Teaching Assistant in Psychology, Ball State University,** Muncie,
                     Indiana.  Graded exams, loaded computers, and helped students
                     having problems with educational software.

## ACTIVITIES AND INTERESTS

1/89-5/89:           Volunteered for an autistic child using the Sun-Rise Program.

Johanna Brown
133 Lincoln Drive
Detroit, MI 48099
(613) 555-3361

POSITION DESIRED      Health Care Administrator in a hospital or clinic.

EDUCATION      Master of Science Degree, April, 1972, Western Michigan University, Public Health Administration. Bachelor of Science Degree, April, 1968, Western Michigan University.
Major:  Business.
Minor:  Biology.

EXPERIENCE      1972-1993:  Director, Vicksburg Community Hospitals. Responsible for the operation of the entire hospital: financial planning, personnel, medical activities, and plant.

1971-1972:  Assistant Director, Vicksburg Community Hospitals.  Handled inpatient and outpatient admittance, cost control, and emergency services.

1968-1971:  Assistant Director, Plainwell Community Hospitals.  Managed billing practices, cost control, and new cost procedures.

COMMUNITY
SERVICE      Volunteer Firefighter in Vicksburg, 8 years.  Member of the committee to study the emergency care facilities in Vicksburg.

RELEVANT
INFORMATION      Participated in professional in-service seminars such as:  cost control, financial planning, billing and collection systems, inpatient admittance, and Lynn Hall's lecture series relating Occupational Therapy to the hospital environment.

Member of the American Public Health Association and American Academy of Hospital Administrators.

Evelyn Moore
4366 South Street
Detroit, MI 48062
(616) 555-9698


**Career Goal:** To obtain a position teaching dental hygiene.

**Education:** September, 1986 - June, 1988

Temple University, Philadelphia, PA
M.S. Dental Hygiene

September, 1981 - June, 1986

Western Michigan University, Kalamazoo, MI
B.S. Dental Hygiene

September, 1976 - June, 1981

Littlefield Public School, Albert, MI
Graduated salutatorian

**Work Experience:** June, 1988 - Present

Dental Hygiene Department of Western Michigan University. Kalamazoo, MI. Phone: (613) 555-4620. Instructor. Classes: oral anatomy, periodontology, and physiology.

September, 1986 - April, 1988

Dental Hygiene Department of Western Michigan University. Kalamazoo, MI. Phone: (613) 555-1244. Graduate Assistant. Duties: teaching section in periodontology and physiology, grading assignments and quizzes, and recording attendance for lecture periods.

**References:** Available upon request.

Stephanie Johnson
5024 Orinda Lane
Indianapolis, Indiana 64022
(317) 555-9601

GOAL:            To be a dental hygienist in a family practice.

EDUCATION:       MARIAN COLLEGE - Associate Degree in Dental Hygiene, 1985

                 CATHEDRAL HIGH SCHOOL - Honors Diploma, 1983

EMPLOYMENT:      ROBERT REYNOLDS, D.D.S.
                 8629 Weber Street
                 Indianapolis, Indiana 46022

                 Hygienist, 1989 to present

                 • Examine teeth and gums.
                 • Clean and polish teeth.
                 • Take and develop x-rays.
                 • Screen patients for oral cancer.
                 • Give fluoride treatment.
                 • Instruct patients in home oral health procedures.

                 AMANDA LINDSAY, D.D.S.
                 4825 Ridge Road
                 Indianapolis, Indiana 46040

                 Dental Assistant and Hygienist, 1985 to 1989

                 • Take and develop x-rays.
                 • Make preliminary impressions for study casts.
                 • Participate in "four-hand procedures."
                 • Prepare filling materials and cements.
                 • Take impressions.
                 • Keep the patient's mouth comfortable.

REFERENCES:      Available on request.

# CURRICULUM VITAE

NAME:          Jill MacFarlan                    TELEPHONE:        416 555 5739

OBJECTIVE:     To obtain a position as pharmacist in a retail drugstore.

EDUCATION:

1987 - Present    University of Toronto

4th Year          BSc Pharmacy Honors
                  Course involves:   Pharmaceutics, Drugs and Disease,
                  Pharmaceutical Chemistry, Clinical Pharmacy.

EMPLOYMENT HISTORY:

-PROCURATOR FISCAL'S OFFICE, Summer 1991-

This mainly involved clerical duties and dealing with telephone enquiries from the public.
The position was useful in that I had to use a computer and deal with the public.

-LADBROKES RACING LTD, Summer 1992-

In this job, I worked as a cashier and became accustomed to handling money quickly and
accurately.  This job helped me develop experience in dealing with members of the
public -- it was important to be polite, helpful, and tactful, skills which are important in
pharmacy.

-ASDA STORES LTD, Present-

This job was taken to give me extra funds and is mainly on Sundays.  I am employed as a
check-out operator where again I deal with the public.  My work experience is beneficial
in showing me how to establish good working relationships with colleagues.

## LEISURE INTERESTS:

At school, I was involved in the Justice and Peace Group and the Children's Fund which entailed taking handicapped and underprivileged children on outings and holidays. I found this enjoyable and very rewarding.

I have organized fundraising activities for several charities, such as an adoption society. This helped me to develop organizational skills, while helping worthwhile causes. I was a youth club leader and was responsible for groups of young people on various outings.

In my spare time at University, I enjoy reading, listening to music, and creative dressmaking. I try to keep fit with various sports, such as badminton. I attend many RPSGB seminars, which I find both interesting and informative.

## REFERENCES:

Dr. Daniel Wright, Lecturer
c/o Pharmacy Department
University of Toronto
Toronto, Ontario

Mr. Richard Woerner, Pharmacist
86 Inveroran Drive
Toronto, Ontario

NAME:                          Jane R. Reynolds

ADDRESS:                       1241 Rue Louis XVI
                               St. Leonards
                               Montreal, Quebec

TELEPHONE NUMBER:              514-555-1926

SECONDARY SCHOOL/UNIVERSITY ATTENDED:

St Bride's High School         from 1982 to 1988
Concordia University           from 1988 to 1992

EXAMINATIONS ACHIEVED:

English, Mathematics, Biology, Chemistry, Higher grade B, 1987.
Certificate of SYS Chemistry, grade A, 1988.

THIRD YEAR SUMMER GRADES IN PHARMACY BSc COURSES:

Pharmaceutical Chemistry       83%
Pharmaceutics                  57%
Pharmacy Practice              74%
Drugs and Disease              70%
Drug Disposition and
  Biopharmaceutics             84%

EMPLOYMENT DURING THE SUMMERS OF 1989, 1990, 1991:

Name of Employer:              Robert G. Gross, MRPharmS
Position Held:                 Dispenser

ACTIVITIES:                    Keeping fit, reading, listening to music.  Member,
                               Sports Union, Concordia University.

REFERENCES:                    Joy Fisher, MRPharmS      Dr. James Travers
                               96 Calderwood Square      Department of
                               Montreal, Quebec          Pharmacology
                                                         Concordia University
                                                         Montreal, Quebec

CURRICULUM VITAE


Alan Frederick Smith, M.D.
Associate in Medicine
Department of Nephrology
Co-Director of Dialysis Center, VA Hospital


Address:                    8 Dunmore Court
                            Durham, North Carolina 27713
                            (919) 555-0918

                            Box 3036
                            Division of Nephrology
                            Duke University Medical Center
                            Durham, North Carolina 27710
                            (919) 555-5043


Degrees:                    B.S., Biomath, Union College, 1983
                            M.D., Duke University, 1987

Spouse:                     June Smith, M.D.
                            BC:  Internal Medicine
                            BE:  Endocrinology

Child:                      Deborah Smith, 12/31/91

Education:                  Duke University School of Medicine, Durham, NC
                            Nephrology Fellowship, 1990-1993
                            Board Eligible Nephrology
                            Internal Medicine Internship and Residency,
                            1987-1990

Research Experience:

July 1991-Present           Duke University Medical Center, Department of
                            Nephrology, Joseph P. Major, M.D. - Clinical
                            trials and basic lab research on metallic
                            bone disease.

Aug 1985-May 1986           Durham VA Hospital, Duke University Medical
                            Center, Renal Physiology Laboratory,
                            Department of Medicine, Mark George, M.D. and
                            Carl Kline, M.D. - Relating products of renal
                            arachidonic acid metabolism to mechanisms of
                            cell injury and cell death.

Curriculum Vitae
Alan Frederick Smith, M.D.
Page 2


| Summer 1982 | SUNY, Stony Brook, NY, Department of Surgery, Richard Alden, M.D. - Ten-year retrospective study of postoperative complications and failure rate of herniorrhaphy at SUNY Stony Brook, NY, Surgical Hernia Clinic. |
|---|---|
| Specialty Board Certification: | Board Certified Internal Medicine, 1991 |
| Licensure: | North Carolina License of Medicine, 1990 |
| Research Support History: | National Institutes of Health - Training Grant Research Award, 1991-1992 |

Honors:    Magna Cum Laude, Union College
AOA Symposium Poster Presentation, Duke
University Medical Center
Assistant Chief Resident, Duke University
Medical Center, April-June 1990
- Supervised the residency program at Durham
  Regional Hospital, Durham, NC
- Prepared Grand Rounds at Durham Regional
  Hospital, Durham, NC
- Prepared morbidity and mortality
  conferences and journal club for the
  Department of Medicine, Duke University
  Medical Center
- Taught Physical Diagnosis classes for Duke
  University Medical Students
- In-service in the ICUs on CAVHD

Special Interests:    Tennis
Downhill Skiing
Skeet Shooting

## CURRICULUM VITAE

Monica Rodrigez, M.D.

Address:

5092 Ilo Drive
Indianapolis, IN 46220
(317) 555-8000 Work
(317) 555-2989 Home

EDUCATION:

Undergraduate:

Walsh College
Canton, Ohio
Bachelor of Arts - double major in biology and chemistry, 1984

Graduate:

Indiana University
College of Medicine
Indianapolis, Indiana
Medical Doctor, 1988

Postgraduate:

Indiana University Hospital
Indianapolis, Indiana
Internal Medicine Internship, 6/88-6/89
Internal Medicine Residency, 6/89-6/91
Nephrology Fellowship, 6/91-6/93

CERTIFICATIONS:

National Board of Medical Examiners Certificate
State Medical License for Indiana, 1989
American Board of Internal Medicine, 1991

## CURRICULUM VITAE

Monica Rodrigez, M.D.

ACADEMIC HONORS AND AWARDS:

Valedictorian Walsh College, G.P.A. 4.0
Walsh College Academic Scholarship
Three Walsh College Honors Certificates
Outstanding Junior Chemist from Walsh College in Akron Section of the American Chemical Society
Letter of Commendation in Internal Medicine
Letter of Honors in Family Medicine
Veterans Association Award for Outstanding Performance at the Veterans Clinic in Indianapolis, Indiana

PROFESSIONAL ORGANIZATIONS:

American Medical Association
Indiana Medical Association

GRANTS:

National Kidney Foundation of Indiana Affiliate, Mechanisms of Glomerular Injury: Lipid Induced Production of Monocyte Chemotactic Factory by Cultured Mesangial Cells, 1992-1993.

RESEARCH:

Compiled drug elution time tables with capillary gas chromatographs at Accutox Toxicology Laboratory, 1983-1984.

REFERENCES:

Robert A. Newman, M.D.
Chairman, Division of Nephrology
Professor, Internal Medicine
N210 Means Hall, 1654 Upham Drive
Indianapolis, IN  46200 (3l7) 555-4997


Joseph J. Jones, M.D.
Division of Nephrology
Associate Professor, Internal Medicine
N210 Means Hall, 1654 Upham Drive
Indianapolis, IN  46200 (317) 555-2345

## CURRICULUM VITAE

| | |
|---|---|
| **Name** | Gordon A. Rosin<br>Major, United States Army |
| **Present Position** | Assistant Chief Nurse Anesthetist<br>Bradley Army Community Hospital<br>Ft. Worth, TX 75000 |

1. **Personal Background**

   a.   Born Columbus, OH

   b.   Penn High School 1971

2. **Educational Background**

   | Troy State University | Texas Wesleyan University |
   |---|---|
   | Troy, AL | Ft. Worth, TX |
   | BSN  1980 | MS  1987 |

3. **Military Schools and Courses**

   a.   Clinical Specialist Course 91C
        Army Medical Department
        William Beaumont Army Medical Center
        El Paso, TX  1974

   b.   Medical Field Service School
        Academy of Health Sciences
        Fort Sam Houston, TX  1981

   c.   AMEDD Officers Advanced Course E-23
        Academy of Health Sciences
        Fort Sam Houston, TX  1983

   d.   Combined Officers Advanced Staff Services School
        Fort Leavenworth, KS  1986

   e.   Academy of Health Sciences
        School of Anesthesiology
        For Army Nurse Corps Officers phase-I
        Fort Sam Houston, TX  1987

f.    Academy of Health Sciences
School of Anesthesiology
For Army Nurse Corps Officers phase-II
Darnell Army Community Hospital
Fort Hood, TX  1988

g.    AMEDD Officers Clinical Head Nurse Course
Academy of Health Sciences
Fort Sam Houston, TX  1988

**4.    Licenses**

a.    Registered Nurse, Alabama, 1980 #5-55555

b.    Registered Nurse, Texas, 1989 #555555

c.    Certified Registered Nurse Anesthetist, 1989 #55555

d.    Registered Nurse, Indiana, 1991 #55555555

**5.    Professional Societies**

American Association of Nurse Anesthetists, 1989

**6.    United States Army Service**

a.    Assistant Chief Nurse Anesthetist
Bradley Army Community Hospital
Fort Worth, TX
1991-Present

b.    Staff Nurse Anesthetist
Operation Desert Shield/Storm
2nd Mobile Army Surgical Hospital
Fort Benning, GA
1990-1991

c.    Staff Nurse Anesthetist
William Beaumont Army Medical Center
El Paso, TX
1989-1991

d.  Staff Nurse NICU/ICU
121st Evacuation Hospital
Yongsan, Korea
1985-1986

e.  ER/ICU Charge Nurse, E/N Supervisor
Lyster Aeromedical Center
Fort Rucker, AL
1981-1985

f.  Staff/Charge Nurse Float
ICU/SICU/CVSU/CCU
St. Margaret Hospital
Montgomery, AL
1979-1981

g.  Staff Nurse RN/LPN ER/ICU/MS
Edge Memorial Hospital
Troy, AL
1976-1979

h.  Staff Nurse LPN  ER
Springhill Memorial Hospital
Mobile, AL
1975-1976

7.  **Civilian Experience**

a.  Obstetric Anesthesia Part-time
Vista Hills Medical Center
El Paso, TX
1989-1991

b.  Obstetric Anesthesia Part-time
Sierra Medical Center
El Paso, TX
1989-1990

c.  Staff Nurse Ortho/ICU Part-time
Jackson Hospital
Montgomery, AL
1979-1981

## Resume
### of
**Pauline S. Birch**
1610 Willow Lane
New Haven, KY  57220
(613) 555-1583

**POSITION DESIRED:**  School Psychologist

**EDUCATION:**  North Salem University - B.A., Psychology (1974)

Bellaire University - M.A., Psychology (1982)

Williamshire University - Ed.S., School Psychology (1991)

**CERTIFICATION:**  School Psychologist I

**WORK EXPERIENCE:**

6/90 - 8/91  Williamshire University Counseling & Testing Clinic/Department

Position:  Graduate Assistant (20 hrs/wk)

4/87 - 3/90  Kramer Clinic

Position:  Addictions  Counselor

12/83 - 4/87  Children's Services

Position:  Counselor

11/78 - 12/83  Comp-tek, Inc.

Position:  Office Manager

**MEMBERSHIPS/
OFFICES HELD:**  Williamshire University Graduate Council, Student Representative

Association of Graduate Counselors at Williamshire University, Vice President

David Edward Garcia
17644 Ventura Blvd.
Los Angeles, CA   90024
(213) 555-9876

PERSONAL DATA   -- --        Excellent communication skills in
                             English and Spanish


EDUCATION       -- --        A.A., Riverside Junior College
                             Riverside, CA


EMPLOYMENT      -- --        <u>Southern California Laboratories</u>,
                             Los Angeles, CA
                             August, 1989 - February, 1993
                             Medical Laboratory Technician


                             <u>U.C.L.A. Outpatient Clinic</u>,
                             Los Angeles, CA
                             June, 1988 - July, 1989
                             Medical Laboratory Technician


                             <u>Lowell Pharmaceuticals</u>,
                             Riverside, CA
                             May, 1986 - May, 1988
                             Medical Laboratory Technician


ADDITIONAL
  EXPERIENCE    -- --        Registered Laboratory Technician


PROFESSIONAL
  ORGANIZATIONS -- --        International Society for Clinical
                             Laboratory Technology


REFERENCES      -- --        Available on Request

Patrick R. Collen
876 West 9th Street
Connersville, IN 47331
(317) 555-9240


OBJECTIVE:     TO GAIN A POSITION IN NUTRITIONAL CARE.


EDUCATION:     M.S. IN NUTRITION, Wabash College
Crawfordsville, IN, 1981

B.S. IN DIETETICS, Wabash College
Crawfordsville, IN, 1979


EXPERIENCE:

August '86 -
Present              Dietary Director, Wabash Hospital, Wabash, IN.
                     Supervise in-depth nutritional assessment of patients on
                     hyperalimentation and formation of classes on weight
                     reduction, diabetes, and geriatric nutrition.

May '85 -
July '86             Consultant Dietitian, (part-time) Veterans Hospital, Indianapolis, IN.
                     Developed standards for nutritional care.

April '81 -
August '84           Clinical Dietitian, St. Mary's Hospital, South Bend, IN.
                     Created cost-effective nourishment center. Established
                     nutritional care standards for individuals with HIV Virus for
                     use by local dietitians.


ADDITIONAL
INFORMATION:    *     Enjoy skiing, running, and volleyball
                *     Orchestra member
                *     Fluent in German, proficient in French

# CURRICULUM VITAE

| | | | |
|---|---|---|---|
| **NAME:** | ALICIA ALVAREZ | **DATE:** | FEBRUARY 18, 1993 |

**PRESENT**
**ADDRESS:** 9867 HIGH DRIVE       **PHONE:**    (606) 555-0000
               LEXINGTON, KY 40506

**OBJECTIVE:** A position as a respiratory therapist with a hospital interested in using my skills as a technical resource person. Possibility for move into management as department director preferred.

**EDUCATION:**

6/83 - 6/85       LOUISIANA TECH INSTITUTE, Ruston, LA.
Associate Degree in Respiratory Therapy.

**EXPERIENCE:**

4/89 - present       LEXINGTON GENERAL HOSPITAL, Lexington, KY.
Respiratory Therapist.
Supervised staff respiratory technicians. Served as resource person for hospital staff.

7/85 - 3/89       KENTUCKY CLINIC, Lexington, KY.
Respiratory Therapist.
Participated in the diagnosis, evaluation, and prevention of respiratory problems.

**ADDITIONAL**
**INFORMATION:**       Member, AARC
Registered Respiratory Therapist

RESUME OF QUALIFICATIONS
OF
PATRICIA WHITE

987 West 44th Street
Cheyenne, WY 82001
(307) 555-9872

## PROFESSIONAL OBJECTIVE

Opportunity to demonstrate superior managerial ability and administrative decision-making skills in a nursing home environment.

## SUMMARY OF QUALIFICATIONS

- Highly organized and motivated.

- Ability and patience to train and develop office and professional staff.

- Thorough knowledge of computers - IBM PC, Lotus 1-2-3, WordPerfect, Symphony Data Base, IBM 38, typing, 10-key by touch, dictaphone, and 2-way radio system.

- Extensive experience in all phases of geriatric care: management, accounting, and medical treatment.

- Good rapport with all levels of employees, patients and their families, and public agencies.

## EDUCATION

University of Wyoming, B.A. Business
Laramie, WY

## EXPERIENCE

1985-Present - Assistant Director, Longview Manor, Cheyenne, WY

1983-1985 - Business Manager, Mountain Top Nursing Home, Cheyenne, WY

## REFERENCES

Excellent professional and personal references

Samuel Ho
9845 Corning Drive
Denver, CO 80233
(303) 555-9347

| | |
|---|---|
| OBJECTIVE: | A position as ombudsman in a large teaching hospital. |
| EDUCATION: | Boston University, Boston, Massachusetts, M.S., Health Advocacy, 1986 |
| | Saint John's College, Annapolis, Maryland, B.A., Psychology, 1982 |

EXPERIENCE:

| | |
|---|---|
| 6/90-PRESENT | **Boston HMO**, Boston, Massachusetts. Individualizing health care for patients and conducting sensitivity training sessions for staff members. |
| 6/87-6/90 | **St. John's Hospital**, Annapolis, Maryland. Resolved problems of individual patients, especially the elderly, and secured appropriate post-hospitalization services for patients. |
| 4/86-4/87 | **Cambridge Nursing Center**, Cambridge, Massachusetts. Acted on behalf of indigent patients. |

ADDITIONAL
INFORMATION:

| | | |
|---|---|---|
| | **Computer Skills:** | WordPerfect, Lotus 1-2-3 |
| | **Foreign Language:** | Chinese |

AFFILIATIONS:    American Psychology Association

National Society for Patient Representation and Consumer Affairs of the American Hospital Association

## MARY ELLEN BOYD

Current Address:
P.O. Box 45
Medford, MA 02155
(617) 555-6543

Permanent Address:
65 Fairbanks Drive
Carmel, IN 46032
(317) 555-9843

### OBJECTIVE

To obtain a position as a respiratory therapist utilizing my experience in the long-term treatment of geriatric patients.

### EDUCATION

Medford Technical School, Medford, MA
September 1988 - March 1990

### RELEVANT COURSE WORK

Biology, Chemistry, Physics
Physiology
Airway Management, Pharmacology
Gas, Aerosol, and Humidity Therapy
Pulmonary Rehabilitation
Cardiopulmonary Anatomy
Stress Analysis
Software Engineering
Mechanical Ventilation
Ethnics of Respiratory Therapy
Systems and Disorders of Breathing

### EXPERIENCE

Respiratory Therapist
March 1990 - Present
Humana Hospital, Medford, MA

Perform tests to evaluate and diagnose respiratory problems. Develop preoperative visitation program for surgical patients. Instruct patients in the use of respiratory treatment aids and methods.

### ADDITIONAL INFORMATION

*Registered Respiratory Therapist

*Free to Relocate

Paula Thomas
974 Chestnut Hill Road
Newark, DE 19713
(302) 555-9812

QUALIFICATIONS      Ten years experience in Medical Social Work
in a hospital environment

Certified Social Worker

EDUCATION      Master's degree in Social Work
University of Delaware, Newark, Delaware, 1982

Bachelor's degree in Social Work
University of Delaware, Newark, Delaware, 1979

Honors Diploma - Newark High School
Newark, Delaware, 1975

Rotary Exchange Student - Germany, 1974

Various A.C.S.W. Seminars

WORK EXPERIENCE

10/86-Present      Atlantic Hospital
Newark, Delaware

<u>Leader of the Hospital Health Team</u>

Coordinated the services of doctors, nurses,
and other hospital health care professionals
to insure that all resources are employed in
the recovery of individual patients.

<u>Supervisor of the Pediatric Unit</u>

Helped ease fears of parents and children
about patients' medical condition. Conducted
family assessments. Referred parents to
appropriate community services.

1982-10/86          Chocorus Community Hospital
                    Chocorus, New Hampshire

                    <u>Community Health Services Coordinator</u>

                    Found homes for children without caretakers
                    because of parental hospitalization. Helped
                    elderly who needed nursing assistance in their own
                    homes. Educated patients on health services
                    available in community. Counseled patients on
                    handling finances and family relationships changed
                    by hospitalization.

INTERESTS           Reading, dressmaking, music

AFFILIATIONS        American Association of University Women

                    Girls' Club of Chocorus

REFERENCES          Available upon request

JOHN J. ALLEN

| Present Address | Permanent Address |
|---|---|
| 765 5th Street | 28 Octavia Terrace |
| Washington, D.C. 20016-8001 | Washington, D.C. 20019 |
| (202) 555-2213 | (202) 555-9737 |

**OBJECTIVE**

Full-time position as a medical writer for a pharmaceutical company, medical school, textbook publisher, or government agency.

**EDUCATION**

George Washington University

Currently pursuing M.S. in technical writing with a concentration in biology.

Whitman College

B.S. with Highest Distinction in English,  May 1990

**EXPERIENCE**

Eli Lily and Company, Indianapolis, IN
Summer 1992

SUMMER INTERN:
Analyzed new product data and prepared reports for in-house use by salesmen.  Interviewed researchers and prepared articles for company publications.

Washington Post, Washington, D.C.
Summer 1991

SUMMER INTERN:
Wrote columns on health fads, fitness, and new drugs.

**ADDITIONAL INFORMATION**

WordPerfect and Word
AMWA certificates in pharmaceutical writing and editing
Member, American Medical Writers Association
Editor, Whitman College newspaper
Enjoy windsurfing, weight training, and Tae Kwon Do

Harold K. Johnson
131 Palm Drive
Valparaiso, IN 46438
(219) 555-2232

SUMMARY          Ten years surgical technologist experience with a proven record of competence. Solid background in supporting operating room team in military hospitals including combat field hospitals. Excellent skills in planning and organizing operating room for a clean surgical environment.

EDUCATION        Associate degree, Surgical Technology
                 Rochester Institute of Technology, Rochester, NY, 1983

CERTIFICATION    Certified Surgical Technologist

WORK EXPERIENCE

1983 - Present   United States Army

                 Operation Desert Storm - Surgical Technology Supervisor
                 Responsible for coordinating efforts of medical technologist, scrub technologist, and circulating surgical technologist. Specialist in orthopedic procedures.

                 Fort Sill Army Hospital - Surgical Technologist
                 Responsible for checking supplies and equipment; draping the sterile field; and operating EKG monitors, lights, and suction machines.

INTERESTS        Fishing, scuba diving, and backgammon

REFERENCES       Available upon request

JILL NELSON

Current Address:                           Permanent Address:
897 Burlingame Avenue                       5311 Rosalind, Apt. # 3
Atlanta, GA 30319                          Calumet City, IL 60409
(404) 555-9112                             (708) 555-9991

| | |
|---|---|
| Objective: | Seeking an applied research & development of manufacturing position in the field of health care products. |
| Education: | M.S. Materials Science & Marketing, Princeton University - May 1992<br>B.S. Mechanical Engineering, University of California - May 1990 |
| Experience: | **Research Assistant**<br>Investigated the micromechanical as well as the macromechanical properties of a ceramic matrix-ceramic fiber composite. Prepared testing specimens, and performed various mechanical testing schemes including three, four point bending and tensile tests. Progress of the research was supervised by Dr. James Worth.<br><br>**Lab Consultant**<br>Helped students debugging programs written in FORTRAN.<br><br>**Research Assistant**<br>Investigated the possibility of two polymer systems being the precursor of a superconducting material. Various compositions of the polymer solutions were prepared and fibers were spun via several methods. High temperature mechanical testings were carried out to determine the survivability of the fiber under pyrolysis. |
| Areas of Interest: | Student member of the American Society of Mechanical Engineers<br><br>Backpacking, travel, photography, and scuba diving |
| References: | Available upon request. |

| | |
|---|---|
| RESUME OF: | Jeffrey Lien |

| | |
|---|---|
| EDUCATION: | B.S. BIOMEDICAL ENGINEERING TECHNOLOGY<br>Purdue University, Lafayette, IN |

EXPERIENCE:

1983 - Present — Whitehall and Miles, Inc.
Honolulu, HI

Member of health and research teams, applying the principles and technologies of various disciplines to the understanding, defining, and solving of medical and biological problems.

Specialized in helping to develop the artificial lung, nuclear magnetic resonance, respiratory and cardiac pacemakers, and plastic heart valves.

Engaged in the analysis and testing of different materials to determine whether they will be accepted or rejected when used in the body in artificial organs and grafts.

ADDITIONAL
INFORMATION: Fluent in Spanish
Working knowledge of German, French, and Italian

ADDRESS: 1908 Greenbay Avenue
Honolulu, HI 96825
(808) 555-9090

REFERENCES: Available on request

PETER MICHAEL JENNINGS, M.D.
114 Laurel Lane
Jamestown, PA  15904
(814) 555-3498

PRESENT PROJECT:

- Private practice in family medicine with special interest in critical care management.
- Consultations at Memorial and Valley Hospitals.

EDUCATION & EXPERIENCE:

July 1990 - Sept. 1991
- Fellow, Department of Critical Care Medicine, Community Hospital, Pittsburgh, PA.

Oct. 1988 - June 1990
- Fellow, Department of Family Medicine, Temple University Hospital, Philadelphia, PA.

July 1987 - Sept. 1988
- Resident, PGY III Internal Medicine, Valley Memorial Hospital, Jamestown, PA.

July 1986 - June 1987
- Resident, PGY II Internal Medicine, Valley Memorial Hospital, Jamestown, PA.

July 1985 - June 1986
- Resident, PGY I Transitional Medicine, Valley Memorial Hospital, Jamestown, PA.

May 1985 - June 1985
- Assistant Resident, Internal Medicine, Valley Memorial Hospital, Jamestown, PA.

July 1984 - Jan. 1985
- Attended the Stanley Kaplan Educational Center, Houston, TX. Self-educational center, involving extensive study of the Basic & Clinical Sciences.

July 1983 - June 1984
- Rotating Resident Internship, Brown Memorial Hospital, Dallas, TX.

Sept. 1979 - May 1983
- Bachelor of Medicine & Bachelor of Surgery, Christian Medical College, Dallas, TX.

PETER MICHAEL JENNINGS, M.D.   - Page 2


AFFILIATIONS:                  - Member, American College of
                                 Physicians (Associate).

LICENSURE:                     - Commonwealth of Pennsylvania,
                                 MD-555555-L, DEA-55555555.
                               - Board Certified in Internal
                                 Medicine by American Board of
                                 Internal Medicine, Sept. 1988.
                               - Board eligible in Family Medicine
                                 by American Board of Internal
                                 Medicine.
                               - Board eligible in Critical Care
                                 Medicine.

## CURRICULUM VITAE

### JASON L. PEABODY, M.D. F.A.C.P.

**Work Address:**                             Kidney Disease Program
                                              James R. Wright University
                                              School of Medicine
                                              690 N. Holland Street
                                              Lexington, KY  40292
                                              Telephone:  (502) 555-9820

**Home Address:**                             8902 Douglas Drive
                                              Lexington, KY  40292
                                              Telephone:  (502) 555-8753

**Academic Title:**                           Professor of Medicine (1989)
                                              Division of Nephrology
                                              Kidney Disease Program
                                              James R. Wright University
                                              School of Medicine
                                              Director of Dialysis Related Services

**Colleges and Universities Attended:**

1969          B.A., Northwestern University, Evanston, IL
1973          M.D., Indiana University of Medicine, Indianapolis, IN

**University or Hospital Appointments:**

1973 - 1974          Rotating Intern:  University of Oregon Health Sciences Center, Portland, OR

1974 - 1976          Residency in Internal Medicine:  University of Oregon Health Sciences Center, Portland, OR

1976 - 1978          Fellowship, Nephrology:  University of Oregon Health Sciences Center, Portland, OR

1978 - 1988          Associate Professor of Medicine:  University of Oregon Health Sciences Center, Portland, OR

**Curriculum Vitae**                                      **Jason L. Peabody, M.D. - 2**

**University or Hospital Appointments (Continued):**

1989 -          Professor of Medicine:  James R. Wright University, Lexington, KY

**Board Certification:**

1976          Internal Medicine
1978          Nephrology

**Licensure:**

Kentucky        (#555555)
Oregon          (inactive)
Washington      (inactive)
Indiana         (#55555555)

**Professional Societies:**

Fellow, American College of Physicians
Chairman, Membership Committee for Oregon ACP Chapter
American Society of Nephrology
Northwest Renal Society
American Society of Artificial Internal Organs
International Society of Blood Purification
American Society of Internal Medicine (House of Delegates)

**Committees:**
                     OREGON
1975 - 1976    Residency Review Committee
1975 - 1976    Pharmacy Committee
1978 - 1985    End-State Renal Disease Committee
1980           Research and Development Safety Subcommittee
1981           Private Practice Plan
1982           Research
1986           HMO-PPO Liaison Committee
1986           Clinical Computing

                     LEXINGTON, KY
1990           Steering, Medical Outcomes
1991           Residency Evaluation Committee

**Elected National Positions:**

Renal Physicians Association Board of Directors, 1986 - 1989
Chairman, Annual Scientific Assembly, 1987
          Reelected to Board 3/92
Tri-State Renal Network (9) Medical Review Board
          Chairman, Data Management Committee
          Chairman, Peritonitis Study Committee

**Curriculum Vitae**                                          **Jason L. Peabody, M.D. -3**

**Other National Positions:**

United States Renal Data System
Renal Community Council
House of Delegates, American Society of Internal Medicine
National Kidney Foundation, Affiliate Relations Committee

**Grant Support:**

Medical Research Foundation of Oregon
Travenol Laboratory
Upjohn Pharmaceutical Company
School of Medicine (University of Lexington)
Miles Laboratory
Department of Medicine (Oregon)

**Active Research Interests:**

Lipid disturbances in patients with kidney disease
Bone marrow responsivity to epoiten
Computing in clinical medicine
Acquired renal cystic disease

**Editorial Advisory or Review Activities:**

Dialysis and transplantation
Archives of Internal Medicine
American Journal of Kidney Diseases
Annual Meeting of the National Kidney Foundation
Peritoneal Dialysis International
The Medical Letter
American Society of Nephrology
ASAIO Transactions
Kidney International
Blood Purification

RESUME
OF
MARK OVERSTREET
1031 116th St.
Indianapolis, IN  46202


OBJECTIVE:    To utilize my professional abilities to obtain a position in the field of nursing.

EDUCATION:    Academy of Health Sciences
              Fort Worth, TX
              EMT/Medical Assistant
              Certificate, 1987

              Gorgas Army Hospital
              Fort Worth, TX
              Enhanced Acute Trauma
              Certificate, 1987

              NCO Academy
              Fort Knox, KY
              3 semester hours, 1990

              Vincennes University
              Vincennes, IN
              General Studies
              34 semester hours, 1991

              Lawrence Fire Department
              EMT Defibulator
              State Certificate, 1991

WORK EXPERIENCE:

1987-1988     U.S. Army; Fort Worth, TX, 5th/87th Infantry
              Emergency Medical Technician
1988          U.S. Army; Fort Worth, TX, Gorgas Army Hospital
              Medical Assistant
1989-1990     U.S. Army; Fort Harrison, IN, Army Hospital
              Medical Assistant/Phlebotomist
1990-1991     U.S. Army; Fort Harrison, IN, Army Hospital
              Nurses Aide
1990-1992     U.S. Army; Fort Harrison, IN, Army Hospital
              Pediatric Clinic

AWARDS:       Good Conduct Medal - U.S. Army - 1987-1990
              Certificate of Achievement - U.S. Army - 1990-1991

REFERENCES:   Available upon request

CURRICULUM VITAE

SCOTT M. FRANK, M.D.

1. PERSONAL DATA

| | |
|---|---|
| Birthplace | Dayton, OH |
| Citizenship | U.S.A. |
| U.S. Social Security # | 555-55-5555 |

| | |
|---|---|
| Home Address | 983 Crestview Drive<br>Osceola, IN  46544<br>(219) 555-9872 |

2. EDUCATION

| Year | Degree | Institution |
|------|--------|-------------|
| 1976 | B.S. | University of Cincinnati |
| 1981 | M.D. | University of Cincinnati,<br>College of Medicine |

3. POSTGRADUATE TRAINING

| Year | Position | Institution |
|------|----------|-------------|
| 1981-84 | Residency,<br>Internal Medicine | East Virginia Graduate School<br>of Medicine, Norfolk, VA |
| 1984-86 | Fellow, Nephrology | University of Iowa Hospitals<br>and Clinics, Troy, IA |

4. PROFESSIONAL EXPERIENCE

| | |
|---|---|
| 1986-Present:  Private<br>Practice in Nephrology,<br>Dialysis, & Transplantation | 8978 Foxworth, Suite 555<br>Osceola, IN  46244<br>(219) 555-2389 |

5. APPOINTMENTS

| | |
|---|---|
| Medical Director:  Dialysis<br>Transplantation<br>September 1991 | Osceola Medical Center<br>Osceola, IN |
| Clinical Assistant Professor<br>January 1991 | Dept. of Internal Medicine<br>University of Osceola<br>Osceola, IN |

6.  **COMMITTEES**

    Pharmacy and Therapeutics      Osceola Medical Center
    Member 1987-1990
    Chairman 1990-Present

    Institutional Review Board     Osceola Medical Center
    Member 1988-1990

    Capital Equipment              Osceola Medical Center
    Member 1991-Present

7.  **CERTIFICATIONS AND LICENSURE**

    <u>Certification</u>

    American Board of Internal Medicine - 3/26/84 - #555555
    Nephrology, American Board Internal Medicine -
    11/11/86 - #555555

    <u>Licensure (current)</u>

    Indiana - 7/2/86 - #555555

Peggy Martin
580 East Main St.
Noblesville, IN 46210

## Degree Details

BS, Pharmacy, Butler University, Indianapolis, IN, 1979

## Previous Experience

1979 - 1984:

Hilton Drug Company
41 High Street
Indianapolis, IN 46208

i)      Pre-registration experience and Assistant Manager, Hilton Drug Company
        (1979 - 1981)

ii)     Relief Manager, Hilton Drug Company (1981 - 1982)

iii)    Manager, Hilton Drug Company (1982 - 1984)


1984 - 1986:

Gillian Griffiths Chemists Ltd.
187 High Street
Indianapolis, IN 46208

Assistant Manager responsible for two stores

1986 - present:

Self-employed Pharmacist working regular days and any extra days for:  Gillian
Griffiths Chemists Ltd.

## Additional Training

Several MRPTG courses attended, including:

Developing Management Skills
Security in the Pharmacy
First Aid

## Hobbies/Interests

Reading
Gardening
Playing the piano
Movies
Sewing

## References

As can be seen from the above, I have gained wide experience in varied retail pharmacy outlets. I enjoy responsibility, have good organizational abilities, and get along well with people both within the profession and with the general public. In support of this, I offer the following reference:

Luke P. Schmidt
444 High Street
Noblesville, IN  46210
(317) 555-9000

I will supply further references if requested.

**Patricia Allen, RRA**
**645 Green Street**
**Bloomington, IN  47403**
**(812) 555 8765**

**Work History**

1989-Present

St. Vincent's Hospital, Indianapolis, IN
Medical Record Administrator.
Implement new system for retrieving medical records.
Develop policies for processing insurance requests.
Analyze patient data for hospital care programs.
Supervise medical record clerks and transcriptionists.
Develop inservice program for medical record clerks.
Evaluate hospital medical record system.

1985-1989

Purdue Clinic, Lafayette, IN
Medical Record Administrator.
Assisted staff in evaluating efficiency of patient medical care.
Analyzed patient health care programs.
Supervised all medical record clerks.

**Education**

1984-1988

Purdue University, Lafayette, IN
Bachelor of Science in Medical Record Administration.
Requirements completed December 1988.
Courses included Anatomy, Medical Record Administration,
Statistics, Disease Classification, Medical Law, Computer Science,
Medical Terminology, and others.

1980-1984

Bloomington High School North, Bloomington, IN
Courses included mathematics, biology, and computer science.
Tennis team, 1980-1984.
Received Outstanding Computer Science Award.

**Certification**

Registered Record Administrator, 1988.

**Peter Joseph Little**
**354 Long Hill Road**
**Middletown, CT   06457**
**(203) 555-9998**

**OBJECTIVE**

Seeking a rewarding and challenging position in medical record administration where I can utilize over ten years of experience in the medical information field.

**EDUCATION**

NATIONAL TECHNOLOGY INSTITUTE        Associate Degree, 1982
Rochester, NY                        Medical Record Technician

**CAREER SUMMARY**

**JOHNSON MEMORIAL HOSPITAL**
Middletown, CT   06457

MEDICAL RECORD TECHNICIAN

December 1990-Present

Started introductory steps in replacing existing PC hardware in client base.  Directed initial stages of development on new software module for insurance companies.  Provided direction to all medical record clerks and medical record transcriptionists.

**DELTA COMMUNITY HOSPITAL**
Indianapolis, IN   46280

MEDICAL RECORD TECHNICIAN

January 1986-November 1990

Responsible for analyzing records, cross-indexing medical information, and reviewing through to the close of sale. Designed and implemented disease coding system.

**COMMUNITY NORTH HOSPITAL**
Indianapolis, IN   46240

MEDICAL RECORD CLERK

August 1982-November 1985

Entered codes in patients' records, maintained registries, and gathered statistics on studies of bed utilization and operating room usage.

Mary Ellen White

| | |
|---|---|
| School Address | Home Address |
| Duke University | 345 Prospect Road |
| P.O. Box 55 | Cleveland, OH  44136 |
| Durham, NC 27706 | (419) 555-9087 |
| (919) 555-9087 | |

## CAREER OBJECTIVE

A position in biomedical engineering with emphasis on developing artificial organs and joints.

## EDUCATION

Duke University
Durham, NC
Master of Science Degree
Graduation Date:  May, 1992

Significant Courses:
Diagnostic and Therapeutic
Devices, Biomaterials,
Biomedical Engineering
Systems and Design, Computer
Systems, Engineering Biophysics, and
Biomechanics

Duke University
Durham, NC
Bachelor of Science Degree
Graduation Date:  May, 1990

## WORK EXPERIENCE

United Technologies
Edinburgh, IN  46124
May, 1991 to September, 1991
- Tested artificial joint materials
- Studied therapeutic devices

Duke University Biomedical Laboratory
Durham, NC
August, 1990 to May, 1991
- Biomaterials tutor

## HONORS AND ACTIVITIES

- Society of Women Engineers
- Phi Sigma Tau engineering sorority
- American Society of Biomedical Engineers

CURRICULUM VITAE
George M. Jefferson, M.D.

Address and Phone:                Martin Laboratory for Clinical
                                    Research
                                  Martin, Ross, and Company
                                  St. Ann's Hospital
                                  Indianapolis, IN  46202
                                  (317) 555-9871

Home Address and Phone:           9802 Allen Lane
                                  Carmel, IN  46032
                                  (317) 555-8466

1.   Education

     Degrees:                     B.S., Oregon State University, 1966
                                  M.D., (cum laude), University of
                                    Oregon Medical School, 1971
                                  M.S., (biochemistry), University of
                                    Oregon Medical School, 1971

     Training:                    Internship (straight medicine),
                                  7/71 - 7/72
                                  Residency (internal medicine),
                                  7/72 - 7/73
                                  Indiana University Medical School
                                  Indianapolis, IN

                                  Fellowship (medical oncology),
                                  7/73 - 7/75
                                  Fellowship (clinical pharmacology),
                                  7/74 - 7/75
                                  National Cancer Institute
                                  National Institute of Health
                                  Pittsburgh, PA

2.   Academic Appointments

     Clinical Pharmacologist (8/75 - present)
     Martin Laboratory for Clinical Research

     Assistant Professor of Medicine (9/75 - 4/80)
     Assistant Professor of Pharmacology (2/78 - 4/80)
     Associate Professor of Medicine (4/80 - present)
     Associate Professor of Pharmacology (4/80 - present)
     Indiana University Medical School, Indianapolis, IN

2

3. Consultantships

   Consultant in Oncology
   Indiana University Medical School

4. Specialty Board Status

   Diplomate, National Board of Medical Examiners,
   Cert. #555555, 1973

   Diplomate, American Board of Medical Oncology,
   Cert. #55555, 1977

5. Licensure and Certifications

   State of Pennsylvania, #555-R, 1973
   State of Indiana, #5555-L, 1975

6. Professional Societies

   Member, American Federation for Clinical Research
   Fellow, American College of Physicians
   Member, C.G. Hangly Institute of Bloomington

7. Honors

   Phi Eta Sigma, 1964
   Phi Kappa Phi, 1966
   Alpha Omega Alpha, 1969

8. Teaching Assignments During the Past Two Years

   Ward Attending Staff, Medicine Service, St. Ann's Hospital,
   1 month per year.
   Duties included supervising and teaching of house staff and
   medical students on clinical clerkships, and attending staff
   responsibility for medicine in-service patients.

   Consultant in Oncology, St. Ann's Hospital,
   1 month per year.
   Duties included supervising fellows in medical oncology,
   teaching senior medical students on elective rotation, and
   formulating treatment plans for inpatients with cancer.
   Fellowship mentor, clinical pharmacology/medical oncology.

9. Professional Activities

   Martin Research Committee Assignments:
   Oncology Action Group (New oncolytics selection)
   Oncology Strategy Working Group

3

10.  Services

University Committee Service - Member, Biostatistics Study
and Planning Committee (Dr. June Reasnor, chairperson)
Four years.

Patient Care Service - Approximately 10% of time spent as
responsible physician in charge of the oncology patients on
the Martin Clinic Service at St. Ann's Hospital. Duties
include direct primary patient care of 5-10 cancer
inpatients and outpatients, some of whom are in a very
advanced state of their disease
Twelve months of the year.

Public Service - In April 1987, participated in an intensive
one week medical mission to the rural people of Haiti,
sponsored by the national organization, LIFELINE, and
Northside Christian Church in Indianapolis.


Signed: _____     Date: _____
        George M. Jefferson, M.D.

## CURRICULUM VITAE

| | |
|---|---|
| Name: | Christine K. Rock |
| Address: | 15 Albert Lane<br>Vancouver, British Columbia<br>Canada |
| Telephone No: | (604) 555-8963 |

| | |
|---|---|
| Qualifications: | Completed 3rd Year of BSC Honors<br>Pharmacy Degree (4 years)<br>Advanced Resuscitation Award SSRL<br>Award of Merit SSRL<br>Duke of Edinburgh Award |

## JOB OBJECTIVE:

To use my pharmacy, communication, and organizational skills in a challenging position as a hospital pharmacist.

## STANDARD/FURTHER EDUCATION:

| | |
|---|---|
| 1988 - Present | University of British Columbia<br>Vancouver, British Columbia |
| 1982 - 1988 | Victoria High School<br>Vancouver, British Columbia |

## SUBJECTS STUDIED:

3rd Year
Fundamentals of Pharmacology; Pharmaceutical Chemistry III, IV, & V; Pharmacy Practice; Biopharmaceutics and Drug Disposition; Drugs & Disease; and General Practice of Pharmacy.

**2nd Year**
Statistics, Pharmaceutics I, Physiology I & II, Pharmaceutical Chemistry I & II, and Interpersonal Skills.

**Ist Year**
Physical, Organic, and Inorganic Chemistry; Bioscience; Pharmaceutical Science and Drug Development; Applications and Implications of Computers; and Marketing for Pharmacists.

## PREVIOUS EXPERIENCE

## DATES

| | |
|---|---|
| July 1991 - Sept 1991 | Rupert Group Research Limited. |
| June 1991 | Prince Edward Hospital.<br>Assigned to follow a tutor for a week, thus being involved in all aspects of Hospital Pharmacy. |
| June 1989 - June 1991 | Fraser Pharmacy.<br>Vacation and Saturday Work.<br>Involved in all aspects of a community pharmacy. Dealt with customers at medicine and cosmetic counters. Prepared and endorsed prescriptions. |
| Dec 1988 - June 1989 | Vancouver Regional Council.<br>Activity Specialist (Lifeguard) at a Local Youth Club.<br>Carried out safety precautions and instructed staff in the proper use of equipment. |
| June 1987 - Sept 1987 | Rosedale District Council.<br>Lifeguard.<br>Supervised public swimming and sunbathing at an outdoor pool. |

## HOBBIES AND INTERESTS

Member of Pharmacy Club, Intramural Badminton Team, and Member of Guides for four years.

## REFERENCES

Available upon request.

# JANE P. WHITLOCK

## HOME ADDRESS

5 Maple Street
South Bend, IN  46237
(219) 555-7892

## JOB OBJECTIVE

To acquire a clinical position in a Physical Therapy facility emphasizing Orthopaedics and Sports Medicine, while continuing to develop my interest in occupational therapy.

## EXPERIENCE

Memorial Hospital, 634-bed acute care facility, 6/89-present.
Staff therapist with responsibilities for managing outpatient department.  Worked closely with a neurosurgeon in developing an exercise program for post-op patients.

Nappanee Hospital, 254-bed acute care facility, 3/87-6/89.
Responsible for inpatient and outpatient physical therapy care with participation in a Sports Medicine Clinic.  In addition, handled burn and multiple-trauma patients.

## EDUCATION

University of Ohio, Bachelor of Science in Physical Therapy, 1987

## PROFESSIONAL ORGANIZATIONS

Member, American Physical Therapy Association

## REFERENCES

Available upon request.

## SUSAN MARIE COOPER
## 111 CENTRAL AVENUE
## INDIANAPOLIS, IN 46268
## (317) 555-9087

EMPLOYMENT

3/86 - Present

Occupational Therapy Department
Indiana Hand Center
Indianapolis, IN 46237
Staff Occupational Therapist, Registered

1/82 - 3/86

Occupational Therapy Department
St. Joseph Medical Center
South Bend, IN 46637
Staff Occupational Therapist

1/79 - 1/82

Occupational Therapy Department
Elkhart Memorial Hospital
Elkhart, IN 46417
Occupational Therapy Assistant

EDUCATION

University of Indiana, 1979
Degree: Bachelor of Science in Occupational Therapy
Cumulative GPA: 3.6    Major GPA: 3.93

SPECIAL PROJECTS

Private Practice: Pediatrics, Independent Study

AFFILIATIONS

American Occupational Therapy Association
Indiana Occupational Therapy Association

REFERENCES

Available Upon Request

DONNA A. POWELL
555 W. Scott Street
Indianapolis, IN  46628
(317) 555-8972


JOB OBJECTIVE        Working in a neonatal nursery as a
                     Clinical Specialist involved in the
                     clinical support of infants and
                     children.


EDUCATION

1990                 Bachelor of Science in Nursing.
                     Purdue University
                     Lafayette, IN
                     Graduated with honors.


EXPERIENCE           Wishard Hospital, Indianapolis, IN.
                     June 1990 to Present.
                     Position:  Staff nurse in the neonatal
                     intensive care unit.


AFFILIATIONS         Indiana Nurses Association
                     National Association of Neonatal Nurses


INTERESTS            Camping, travel, cycling

PAM T. PHILLIPS
444 MULBERRY STREET
CARMEL, IN 46032
(317) 555-7624

## JOB OBJECTIVE

To work in a neonatal nursery as a specialist in clinical care, and to prepare parents for the type of care their babies will need when released from the hospital.

## EDUCATION

| 1988 | University of Michigan<br>Ann Arbor, MI<br>Master of Science in Nursing with a minor in education |
| 1985 | University of Michigan<br>Ann Arbor, MI<br>Bachelor of Science in Nursing |

## WORK EXPERIENCE

1988 - present    Providence Children's Hospital
Indianapolis, IN
Position: Staff Nurse
- create and execute special media presentations for parents of special care infants.

- perform special nursing skills associated with caring for intensive care infants.

1985 - 1988    University of Michigan Medical Center
Ann Arbor, MI
Position: Staff Nurse

## AFFILIATIONS

National Association of Neonatal Nurses

## REFERENCES

Available upon request

ANN GOEBLE
666 Central Avenue
Bay City, IN  46200
(219) 555-8972

JOB OBJECTIVE

To provide quality nutritional care to individuals in nursing homes.

EDUCATION

| | |
|---|---|
| 1985 - 1989 | University of Indianapolis<br>Indianapolis, IN  46200<br>Degree:  B.S. in Dietetics |

EXPERIENCE

| | |
|---|---|
| July, 1991 - Present | **Consultant, Sunset Manor Nursing Home**<br>Indianapolis, IN<br>Develop standards for nutritional care.  Conduct routine clinical duties.  Work as a team member with patients and physicians to build up undernourished patients. |
| June, 1989 - July, 1991 | **Dietetic Assistant, Broadmoor Nursing Home**<br>Indianapolis, IN<br>Worked under dietetic supervisor in helping with menu planning, standardization of recipes, and the ordering of ingredients and supplies.  Assisted patients with menu selections, and wrote basic modified dietary plans for patients. |

PROFESSIONAL SOCIETIES

American Dietetic Association

REFERENCES

Upon request

Robert J. Zimmerman
3897 Washington Blvd.
Noblesville, IN  46620
(317) 555-3467

**Career Goal:**     To obtain a position as a medical illustrator

**Education:**     September, 1990 - June, 1992

University of San Diego
San Diego, CA
M.A., Medical Illustration in Art

Courses studied included drawing, layout, photography,
illustration techniques, zoology, physiology,
chemistry, biology, and histology.

GPA 3.74

September, 1985 - June, 1990

University of Arizona
Tucson, AZ
B.S., Zoology

Courses studied as an undergraduate included a strong
concentration of science courses with an emphasis on
art.

Overall GPA 3.53 - Major GPA 3.8

September, 1980 - June, 1985

Noblesville High School
Noblesville, IN

**Experience:**     Noblesville Topic Daily Newspaper
Noblesville, IN
1985 - 1990 (Summers)

Duties:     Worked in the illustration department at a
variety of tasks and in the layout design
department.

**References:**     Available upon request

Michelle A. Harmon
339 Lexington Place
Carmel, IN  46032
(317) 555-8962

OBJECTIVE:  BIOMEDICAL ENGINEER
To work as member of health and research teams

EDUCATION
Purdue University
Bachelor of Science, Biomedical Engineering, June 1991

RELATED COURSE WORK
Biomedical Engineering
Biomedical Computers
Engineering Biophysics
Bioinstrumentation
Biomechanics
Biotransport
Artificial organs

EXPERIENCE
Butler Williams Inc.
Indianapolis, IN
Bioengineer
1991 to Present

Apply engineering principles to understanding the structure, function, and pathology of the human body.  Also, apply engineering concepts and technology to advance the understanding of biological, nonmedical systems, such as maintaining and improving the quality of the environment and protecting human, animal, and plant life from toxicants and pollutants.

AFFILIATIONS
The International Certification Commission

REFERENCES AVAILABLE UPON REQUEST

Jennifer Bauer
93 West 4th Street
Long Beach, CA 90808
(213) 555-9876

## EDUCATION

June 1990: Bachelor of Science in Cytotechnology, California Institute of Technology, Pasadena, California. GPA 3.65. Related courses of study were bacteriology, physiology, anatomy, histology, embryology, zoology, genetics, chemistry, and computer classes.

## WORK EXPERIENCE

June 1990 - present: **CYTOTECHNOLOGIST**

Circle Center Research Laboratory, Culver City, CA

Duties: To identify cell specimens which are collected by fine needle aspiration and report findings to the pathologist. Use computers to measure cells, a new technique which is being developed at Circle Center Research Laboratory.

## CERTIFICATION

The International Academy of Cytology
National Certification Agency for Medical Laboratory Personnel

## HONORS

Dean's Honor List - Six Times

## REFERENCES

Available upon request

VICTORIA MARIE HOOPER
4678 BRAEWICK DRIVE, INDIANAPOLIS, IN 46236
(317-555-0963)

JOB OBJECTIVE

Seeking a full-time position as a registered nurse with entry into a management position.

EDUCATION

1977: B.S., Nursing, Salve Regina College, Newport, R.I.

SKILLS AND ABILITIES

Public Relations:
- People-oriented
- Chairperson/Coordinator of several Health Fairs
- Health Risk Assessment Coordinator
- Health related counseling/screening

Management:
- Eleven years as a Navy Nurse (1977-1988) managing subordinates (corpsman and junior nurses)
- Chairperson of several hospital/nursing related committees
- Charge Nurse responsibilities in a multifaceted Family Practice Clinic
- Dual role as Nursing Education/Patient Education Coordinator

WORK EXPERIENCE

| | | |
|---|---|---|
| Nov 1977 | Commissioned, Navy Nurse Corps | |
| Dec 1977-Feb 1981 | Great Lakes Naval Hospital | Staff Nurse - Orthopedics, Pediatrics, Psychology, ICU/RR |
| Mar 1981-Nov 1984 | Jacksonville Naval Hospital | Staff Nurse - Medicine Asst. Charge Nurse - Pediatrics |
| Nov 1984-June 1986 | Portsmouth Navy Hospital | Staff Nurse - Pediatric Acute Care Clinic |
| June 1986-Dec 1988 | Orlando Naval Hospital | |
| | June 1986-Sept 1986 | Staff Nurse - MED/Surgical |
| | Sept 1986-Sept 1987 | Charge Nurse - Family Practice Clinic |
| | Sept 1987-Dec 1988 | Nursing - Education/Patient Education/Coordinator |

Victoria Marie Hooper – Page 2

**WORK EXPERIENCE CONTINUED**

| | | |
|---|---|---|
| 15 Dec 1988 | Honorable Discharge from the United States Navy | |
| Dec 1988-Mar 1989 | Engaged in job search | |
| Mar 1989-Present | Fort Benjamin Harrison | Community Health Nurse, Health Promotion Activity |

**REFERENCES**

Available upon request

**PERSONAL RESUME**

**<u>Personal Data</u>**
Pennie Cole Jones
80 Chestnut Street
Minneapolis, MN 55416

Telephone:     Home - (612) 555-8461
                Work - (612) 555-3932

Physical Therapy License:    Minnesota #55555

Social Security Number:    555-55-5555

**EMPLOYMENT EXPERIENCE:**

**AUGUST 1986 TO PRESENT**

Specializing in outpatient neurological and orthopedic diagnoses

Co-owner of Physical Therapy Associates of St. Louis Park.
400 Lakeshore Drive
St. Louis Park, MN 55417

**OCTOBER 1984 TO AUGUST 1986**

Acute rehabilitation, staff therapist

Bloomington Memorial Hospital
Bloomington, MN 55439

**AUGUST 1982 TO JUNE 1983**

Physical Therapy Aide

Minneapolis Rehabilitation Center
Minneapolis, MN 55419

**APRIL 1980 TO JULY 1981**

Physical Therapy Aide

Crestwood Rehabilitation Hospital
Rochester, MN 56214

**OCTOBER 1981 TO APRIL 1982**

Physical Therapy Assistant

St. Paul Rehabilitation Center
St. Paul, MN 55391

**PENNIE COLE JONES**
**RESUME**
**PAGE 2**

**AUGUST 1980 TO AUGUST 1981**

Physical Therapy Aide

Duluth Rehabilitation Hospital
Duluth, MN  54981

**MARCH 1978 TO MAY 1980**

Physical Therapy Aide

Hope Manor Convalescent
St. Cloud, MN  55296

**PROFESSIONAL EDUCATION:**

B.S. Degree in Physical Therapy, University of California, Santa Barbara, 1983-84.
B.A. Degree in Pre-Physical Therapy, minor in Psychology, California State University, Turlock, 1977-80.

**CONTINUING EDUCATION:**

| | |
|---|---|
| April 7-18, 1985 | NDT for Adult Hemiplegia, Certification Course. |
| April 26-28, 1985 | Podiatric Physical Therapy. |
| October 17-20, 1985 | Traumatic Brain Injury Conference. |
| October-April, 1988-89 | Myofascial Strategies I - Larry Peters. |
| October-May, 1989-90 | Myofascial Strategies II - Larry Peters. |
| February 3-4, 1990 | Training Low Back Patient - Michael Monroe. |
| October 28-30, 1991 | The Active Foot Symposium. |
| December 7-8, 1992 | Cranio-Sacral I - Susan Fevre. |

Franklin Wu
5391 Southward Plaza
Walnut Creek, CA 94596
(510) 555-9008

**JOB OBJECTIVE:** To obtain a position as a high-level optician in a fast-paced retail store.

**EDUCATION:** Graduated Hayward Community College, Hayward, CA in June of 1986.

Graduated North Central High School, Chicago, IL in June of 1984.

**WORK EXPERIENCE:**

1990 - present  Great Spectacles, Walnut Creek, CA
Management Optician

1988 - 1990  Valley Vision, Pleasanton, CA
Management Optician and Frame Buyer

1986 - 1988  Dublin Optometry, Dublin, CA
File Clerk

**SPECIAL QUALIFICATIONS:** People person; fashion styling experience; knowledge of adjustments, repairs and fittings of glasses and contact lenses.

**CERTIFICATION:** American Board of Optometry Certificate

**CLASSES AND SEMINARS:** Cal-Q Optics to prepare for licensing, 1992
Opti-Fair - annual, three day seminars

**REFERENCES:** George Jones, O.D.
Great Spectacles, (510) 555-8941

Maria Lazar, Optician
Valley Vision, (510) 555-3726

Name:          Marie Farrell       Date:          March 5, 1993

Present
Address:       568 Cowell Lane      Telephone:     (504) 555-9032
               Tulane University
               New Orleans, LA   70118

Permanent
Address:       50 Cass Street       Telephone:     (402) 555-2562
               Omaha, NE   68132

OBJECTIVE:     TO GET A CHALLENGING CLINICAL FELLOWSHIP IN A
               REHABILITATION CENTER WORKING WITH THE ELDERLY.

EDUCATION:     Tulane University, New Orleans, LA.
               Currently, pursuing a Master of Science degree in
               Speech Pathology.  Course work includes
               swallowing, stroke rehabilitation, adult voice
               disorders, and Alzheimer's Disease.  Anticipated
               June 1993.

               University of Nebraska, Omaha, NE.
               B.A., Health Sciences, June 1991.

EXPERIENCE:

Summer 1992    **Prairie Nursing Home.**  Worked as a recreational
               aide developing and implementing programs for the
               elderly.

Summer 1991    **Fort Custer Camp.**  Acted as residential counselor
               for ten hearing-impaired teenagers.

Summer 1990    **West Bear Camp.**  Taught sign language to
               hearing-impaired children.

INTERESTS:     Photography, Swimming, Tennis, and Classical
               Music.

ADDITIONAL
INFORMATION:   Available on request.

Robin Peters
90 Pacific Coast Highway
Malibu, CA  90024
(310) 555-3546

| | |
|---|---|
| Objective: | To obtain a position with an ambulance company, hospital emergency room, or search and rescue team. |
| Education: | Santa Rosa Jr. College, Santa Rosa, CA. Emergency Medical Technician Course 1A Fire Service/Auto Extrication, 12/92 |
| | Sonoma State University, Rohnert Park, CA. B.A. Environmental Studies, 1/92 Included course work in Advanced First Aid, Emergency Care, Physiology, and Psychology. |
| Experience: | Sonoma Life Support, Sonoma, CA. Assisted paramedics and other EMT's on an ambulance, 11/92. |
| | Emergency Room, Santa Rosa Hospital, Santa Rosa, CA. Helped doctors and nurses in patient care, 10/92. |
| | Home Care Program, Sonoma, CA. Nurse assistant for the elderly, 1991. |
| | Marin Conservation Corps, San Rafael, CA. Acted as corps member and driver, summer 1991. |
| Personal Qualifications: | Excellent knowledge of medical terms. Calm in emergency situations. Polite, helpful, and compassionate. |
| License and Certificate: | Red Cross Community CPR Certificate - 1992 Red Cross Advanced First Aid - 1990 |
| Affiliations: | National Parks Conservation Association Sierra Club |
| Interests: | Swimming, hiking, backpacking, and environmental activities. |

| | |
|---|---|
| **Name:** | Maria Black |
| **Address:** | 1419 Cedar Drive  Phone:  (513) 555-8754<br>Dayton, OH 45226 |

**Qualifications:**  Bachelor of Science in Pharmacy, 1993

**School of Pharmacy:**  Dayton University

**Special Award:**  Merrell Dow Dayton School of Pharmacy's Annual Award for Excellence, 1992

**Previous Experience:**

| Hooks Pharmacy<br>Dayton, OH | Summer Student<br>10 weeks, 1992 |
|---|---|
| Royal Hospital<br>Dayton, OH | Summer Student<br>8 weeks, 1991 |
| Ohio Drug<br>Dayton, OH | Saturday Staff<br>9/87-1/92 |

**Present Position:**  Pharmacy Graduate Intern Program
Dayton Community Hospital
Dayton, OH

**Interests:**  My main interest is in clinical pharmacy.

During my intern year, I have attended Dayton University evening classes on clinical pharmacy and an Ohio State University course in ambulance first aid.

**References:**  Available on request.

Roberta J. Stewart
34 King Crossing
Denver, CO 80203
(303) 555-1566


CAREER OBJECTIVE

Desire a position in office management in a medical or dental clinic.


EDUCATION

Denver Technical College, Denver, CO - February, 1979

Completed Dental Assistant/Receptionist Program


Denver Community College, Denver, CO - 1979 - 1993

Completed courses in WordPerfect, Lotus 1-2-3, medical office management, medical terminology, and administrative procedures

Boulder High School, Boulder, CO - June, 1977

Graduated with a major in business


EXPERIENCE

| | |
|---|---|
| 1985 - Present | Denver Dental Clinic, 124 Aspen Way, Denver, CO 80215 |
| | Office Manager: Handle office payroll and all billing for three dentists. Deal with insurance forms. Keep appointment book. |
| 1980 - 1982 | Dr. Leroy Atkins, 470 Rocky Mountain Drive, Boulder, CO 80217 |
| | Receptionist: Kept appointment book and updated records. |
| 1979 - 1980 | Dr. Thomas Marks, 85 Rocky Mountain Drive, Denver, CO 80217 |
| | Dental Assistant: Helped the dentist at chairside and in the lab. Took X-rays. Prepared patients for oral surgery. |

MARK JOHNSON
871 Goble Street
Boca Raton, FL 33431
(407) 555-8765

## Work History

**1989-present**

Clear Speech, Boca Raton, FL
Speech-language pathologist

Evaluation, diagnosis, and treatment of children with speech disorders.

**1988-1989**

Santa Clara County School for the Deaf
San Jose, CA
Speech-language pathologist and sign language instructor.

**1987-1988**

Private practice, Chicago, IL

Specialized in screening of preschoolers for early identification of hearing and speech impaired.

**1984-1987**

Chicago Public Schools, Chicago, IL
Speech-language pathologist

Elementary School District: Early identification of hearing and speech impaired (one year).

High School District: Treatment of mentally and physically impaired students with speech problems, learning disabled, students with English as a second language, and stutterers (one year).

Special Education District: Treatment of hearing impaired (one year).

## Education

**1984**

Northwestern University, Chicago, IL
M.A. Speech Pathology

**1982**

University of Wisconsin, Madison, WI
B.A. Arts and Sciences with speech and hearing specialty

Certification

Certificate of Clinical Competence of the American Speech and Hearing Association, 1985

Professional Affiliations

American Speech and Hearing Association
Florida Speech and Hearing Association
Greater Boca Raton Speech and Hearing Association

Special Qualifications

Can sign fluently.

ROSEMARIE JOHNSON
232 LEE STREET
DURHAM, NC 27707
(919) 555-6541

## OBJECTIVE

To become a member of the medical staff in a small clinic.

## EXPERIENCE

Registered Nurse          Durham Blood Bank, Durham, NC
                          1988 to present
                          Draw blood, work with autologus
                          program, and take charge of unit when
                          supervisor is absent.

                          The Beck Agency, Durham, NC
                          1986 to 1988
                          Provide long-term care in private
                          homes.

                          Durham General Hospital, Durham, NC
                          1983 to 1986
                          Floor nurse in premature nursery.

## EDUCATION

Bachelor of Science
in Nursing                University of North Carolina, 1983

Refresher Courses         Durham General Hospital, 1983 to 1993
                          Care of premature infants, infant
                          nutrition, behavior modification, and
                          addictive behaviors.

## PERSONAL QUALIFICATIONS

High energy level, excellent health, people-oriented,
knowledge of latest techniques in infant care, and able to be
assertive when necessary.

## CERTIFIED AS A REGISTERED NURSE

North Carolina, 1983

## REFERENCES

Full references will be furnished on request.

PETER SIMMONS
678 PARK STREET #54
PORTLAND, OR 97281
(503) 555-4527

OBJECTIVE:

TO OBTAIN AN EXECUTIVE POSITION IN MARKETING
WITH A MAJOR PHARMACEUTICAL COMPANY DEDICATED
TO THE RESEARCH AND DEVELOPMENT OF NEW DRUGS.

EXPERIENCE:

5/90-PRESENT  COAST PHARMACEUTICALS, PORTLAND, OR 97281
MARKETING DIRECTOR

-DESIGNED MARKETING STRATEGIES FOR LOCAL AND
 NATIONAL MARKETS.
-IMPROVED COMPANY SALES BY OVER 25 PERCENT IN A
 12-MONTH PERIOD.
-DEVELOPED SUCCESSFUL MARKETING PROGRAM FOR
 GENERIC DRUGS.

1/89-5/90  CRESTMORE LABORATORIES, NEW YORK, NY 10016
REGIONAL SALES MANAGER

-SET REGIONAL SALES RECORD IN 6 MONTHS.
-EXCEEDED COMPANY GOALS FOR THE 1989 FISCAL
 YEAR.
-DEVELOPED SALES MARKETING PROGRAM FOR THE
 NORTHWEST REGIONAL AREA.

EDUCATION:

9/86-6/88  M.B.A., UCLA, CONCENTRATION IN MARKETING
               DEAN'S LIST - 6 QUARTERS

9/82-6/86  B.A., UNIVERSITY OF OREGON, MAJOR BUSINESS
                               G.P.A. - 3.8/4.0

AFFILIATIONS:

UCLA BUSINESS SCHOOL ALUMNI BOARD
PORTLAND JUNIOR CHAMBER OF COMMERCE

REFERENCES:  AVAILABLE ON REQUEST.

## RITA GARDEN

32 ELLIOTT AVENUE, AUSTIN, TX 78731
(512) 555-5618
NURSING HOME ADMINISTRATOR

### CAREER OBJECTIVE

TO BECOME A REGIONAL ADMINISTRATOR IN A LARGE NURSING HOME CORPORATION.

### EMPLOYMENT HIGHLIGHTS

SIX YEARS OF EXPERIENCE IN THE ADMINISTRATION OF NURSING HOMES IN AUSTIN, TEXAS. HAVE ACTED AS ADMINISTRATOR IN FACILITIES RANGING FROM 60-BEDS TO 175-BEDS, AND IN INTERMEDIATE AND SKILLED CARE NURSING HOMES.

### EXPERIENCE

1989-PRESENT    AUSTIN NURSING HOMES, INC., AUSTIN, TX
       1991:     ADMINISTRATOR, DESERT VALLEY HOME
       1989-91: ASSISTANT ADMINISTRATOR, DESERT VALLEY HOME

1987-1989      GOODWIN NURSING HOMES, INC., AUSTIN, TX
       1989: ADMINISTRATOR, AUSTIN CONVALESCENT HOSPITAL (AN ALZHEIMER UNIT)
       1988: ADMINISTRATOR, SOUTHWEST NURSING HOME
       1987: ASSISTANT ADMINISTRATOR, SOUTHWEST NURSING HOME

### EDUCATION

JUNE, 1987     UNIVERSITY OF TEXAS, AUSTIN, TX
B.S. IN HEALTH SCIENCE (SUMMA CUM LAUDE)

### LICENSE

JUNE, 1987     NURSING HOME ADMINISTRATOR, LICENSE #5555

### SPECIAL QUALIFICATIONS

A PROBLEM SOLVER WHO KEEPS NURSING HOMES IN COMPLIANCE WITH STATE REGULATIONS. A SKILLED SUPERVISOR WHO SETS A CARING TONE FOR FACILITY STAFF AND PATIENTS.

### REFERENCES

REFERENCES COVERING EDUCATION AND ALL JOBS ARE AVAILABLE ON REQUEST.

MARIA SANCHEZ
285 SPRUCE STREET
PITTSBURGH, PA 19103
(412) 555-7896

## EXPERIENCE

6/88-PRESENT

WATER'S EDGE CONVALESCENT HOSPITAL
PITTSBURGH, PA
FULL-TIME NURSING ASSISTANT

INVOLVED IN THE PERSONAL CARE OF GERIATRIC
PATIENTS - ASSIST WITH PERSONAL NEEDS,
CONVERSE WITH PATIENTS, TAKE BLOOD PRESSURE,
TEMPERATURE, AND PULSE AND RESPIRATION RATES.

9/83-6/85

DOUGLAS MACARTHUR HIGH SCHOOL, MANILA,
PHILIPPINES
TEACHER, SPANISH AND ENGLISH

## EDUCATION

1987

PITTSBURGH VOCATIONAL HEALTH SCHOOL
PITTSBURGH, PA
CERTIFIED NURSE ASSISTANT PROGRAM

6/83

B.A. UNIVERSITY OF MANILA, MANILA,
PHILIPPINES,
MAJOR: SPANISH
MINOR: ENGLISH

## LICENSE

1988

CERTIFIED NURSE ASSISTANT, PENNSYLVANIA

## REFERENCE

SUSAN GRAVES, ADMINISTRATOR
WATER'S EDGE CONVALESCENT HOSPITAL
PITTSBURGH, PA 15044
(412) 555-9122

## PERSONAL DETAILS

NAME                          ANDREW FISHER

ADDRESS                       82 South Twelfth Street
                              Grand Rapids, MI 49503

TELEPHONE                     (616) 555-2983

## EDUCATION

I graduated from Grand Rapids High School in
the top 20 percent of my class in 1983.  My courses
included work in the following subjects: biology,
keyboarding, word processing, accounting, and
business law.

## EXPERIENCE

My current job is medical record technician at the
Hillside Nursing Home, a 175-bed skilled care
nursing facility in Grand Rapids where I have worked
for three years.  My primary responsibility is
auditing medical records to make sure the staff has
carried out doctors' orders.

My previous job was at the Nimitz Navy Hospital in
Detroit where I worked for two years as a medical
record technician putting together patients' records
after they left the hospital.

I also worked at the Nimitz Navy Hospital for one
year as a file clerk before becoming a medical
record technician.

## INTERESTS

My special interest is music.  During my junior and
senior years in high school, I played the clarinet
and alto saxophone with the school marching band.
I now play the clarinet with the Grand Rapids
Community Band.  Other interests include genealogy
and skiing.

ANNA L. STEWART
521 Halstead Avenue
Randolph, NJ 07869
(201) 555-4335


EDUCATION

    Rutgers University, New Brunswick, NJ - BSN - May 1983
    Special emphasis on geriatric care

    Continuing education courses, 1983 to Present, 30 units
    Coursework includes nutrition, arthritis, diabetes,
    Alzheimer's disease, and gerontology


EXPERIENCE

Registered Nurse     January 1988 to Present
                   Randolph Convalescent Hospital
                   Randolph, NJ
                   August 1992 to Present - Director of
                     Nurses
                   July 1991 to July 1992 - Assistant
                     Director of Nurses
                   January 1988 to June 1991 - Charge Nurse

                   October 1986 to November 1987
                   Oceanside Convalescent Hospital
                   Atlantic City, NJ
                   Team Supervisor in skilled care unit

                   July 1983 to August 1986
                   Paradise Hospital
                   Trenton, NJ
                   Full-time floater and surgical nurse


LICENSE

                   Certified as registered nurse in New
                   Jersey, License #555555


QUALIFICATIONS

                   7-years of geriatric nursing
                   Demonstrated concern for the well-being
                     of elderly patients
                   Special coursework in gerontology
                   Proven supervisory skills


REFERENCES

                   Available on request

EVAN L. WATERFIELD
1245 Plaza Drive
Youngstown, OH 44512
(216) 555-8989


EDUCATION

June 1984 to January 1986
Ohio Vocational Schools, Inc., Youngstown, OH - completed
practical nursing course

September 1980 to June 1984
John Glenn High School, Columbus, OH - graduated with
first-class diploma


EXPERIENCE

Sleepy Hollow Nursing Home
45 Diamond Lane
Youngstown, Ohio 44513

February 1990 to Present
Director of Staff Development: interview new patients and
their families, review facility patient care plan and revise
when necessary, orient new staff, give in-service workshops
for staff to update knowledge of equipment, medicine, and
changes in facility

February 1988 to January 1990
Director of Nursing: scheduled nursing staff, evaluated
propective patients, and provided orientation for new
patients and their families

February 1986 to January 1988
Staff nurse: passed medicines, gave treatments, and provided
basic nursing care


LICENSE

Licensed Practical Nurse: Ohio license# 55555


REFERENCES

Available on request

PETRA LEVENTHAL
109 Beach Drive
Virginia Beach, VA 23456
(804) 555-9852

OBJECTIVE

To secure a teaching position at a major
medical school

WORK STYLE

Specialist in resolving eating disorders
Skilled in adapting counseling to client
Analytic and versatile thinker
Communicates with clients and parents with warmth
and diplomacy

EXPERIENCE

Alta Vista Hospital, Virginia Beach, VA
1989 to Present
Clinical Psychologist

Established an eating disorder clinic
Counseled over 100 teenagers with eating disorders
Initiated peer counseling program
Developed intern program
Created a program to assess which clients would
require hospitalization

University of Virginia
1988 - academic year
Taught class on eating disorders
Received psychology department's "Excellence in
Teaching Award"

EDUCATION

Ph.D. in Psychology, University of Virginia, 1989
Concentration: eating disorders
M.S. in Psychology, Yale University, 1986
B.A. in Psychology, Georgetown University, 1984
Graduated magna cum laude

PUBLICATIONS

"A Program to Manage the Continuous Hunger of
Bulimics," Journal of Clinical Psychology, March,
1993, pp. 87-102

"The Self-Destructiveness of Eating Disorders,"
Journal of Psychology, January, 1989, pp. 104-112

AFFILIATIONS

Virginia Association of Psychologists, secretary
American Association of Psychologists
Eating Disorder Association of America
Chair of Bulimia group

# Chapter Six

# SAMPLE COVER LETTERS

1090 OAK DRIVE
MADISON, WI 54702


DECEMBER 14, 1992


MERCY HOSPITAL
6225 MAPLE DRIVE
INDIANAPOLIS, IN 46220


TO WHOM IT MAY CONCERN:

THIS LETTER IS IN RESPONSE TO THE ADVERTISEMENT IN THE
*INDIANAPOLIS NEWS* ON FRIDAY EVENING, DECEMBER 13, 1992 FOR
AN EMERGENCY MEDICAL TECHNICIAN.  PLEASE ACCEPT MY RESUME IN
CONSIDERATION FOR THIS POSITION.

WITH A DEGREE FROM THE UNIVERSITY OF WISCONSIN AND FIVE
YEARS OF WORK EXPERIENCE AS A MEDICAL TECHNICIAN AT
COMMUNITY NORTH HOSPITAL IN MADISON, I BELIEVE THAT I AM
SUITED TO YOUR HOSPITAL'S NEEDS.

THANK YOU FOR YOUR TIME.  I LOOK FORWARD TO HEARING FROM YOU
SOON.


SINCERELY,



MARTIN A. GORDON
(715) 555-8954


ENCLOSURE

## Katherine Malloy

50 Central Avenue
Danville, CA   94526


February 8, 1993


Dear Dr. Elena Rodriguez:

Thank you for speaking with me on February 7, 1993, about the dental hygienist opening in your office.  After talking with you, I find that I am very interested in the position.  I would appreciate the opportunity to become a member of your staff.  With my experience and background, I believe that I would be an asset to your office.

Thank you for your time and consideration.  I look forward to hearing from you soon.

Sincerely,


Katherine Malloy
510 Pine Street
San Ramon, CA 94530
(510) 555-5642

209 East Main Street
Philadelphia, PA 19103


March 25, 1993


Saint Vincent's Hospital
635 Medical Drive, Suite 248
Wilkes-Barre, PA 18711


Dear Sir/Madam:


I am interested in applying for full-time employment as
a psychiatric social worker in the Wilkes-Barre area.
As you can see from my resume, I have considerable
experience in working with disturbed adults.

I would like the opportunity to meet with you to discuss
my qualifications.  I feel that I would be a productive
addition to your hospital staff.


Sincerely,



Dorotea P. Russell
(215) 555-9845

P.S.  I am responding to your ad in Sunday's *Citizen Voice*
regarding the position for a psychiatric social worker.

Margaret Morgan
3033 Diamond Drive
Indianapolis, IN 46220
Tel. (317) 555-1881

November 8, 1992

Riley Children's Hospital
5892 Dupont Avenue
Indianapolis, IN 46256

Dear Sir/Madam:

Presently, I am a graduate student at the Indiana University
School of Nursing pursuing an advanced degree in pediatric
nursing education.  I plan to graduate on June 7, 1993.

Due to my prior work experience in education, the staff of
the Indiana University School Placement Office provided me
with the profile of your teaching hospital.

I am extremely interested in obtaining a position in your
medical institution.  In particular, I would like to teach
in the area of neonatology.

My resume has been enclosed for your review.  Please feel
free to contact me if you require additional information.

I am looking forward to hearing from you.

Sincerely,

Margaret Morgan

Enclosure

March 20, 1993

Laura M. Page
1624 Sawbridge Drive
Indianapolis, Indiana 46033

Mr. Andrew Scaruffi
Human Resources
Hancock Memorial Hospital
4499 Burlington Avenue
Madison, Wisconsin 53708

Dear Mr. Scaruffi:

I am writing in response to our telephone conversation about Hancock Memorial Hospital's need for a physical therapist. As we discussed, I am currently working at St. Francis Hospital Center in Indianapolis, but I am looking to relocate to Wisconsin. After seeing your ad in the *Capital Times* and talking to you, I feel that I am qualified to meet your hospital's needs.

Presently, I have a lease on my house in Indianapolis. If I meet the requirements, I am available for employment at any time. I would like to move to Wisconsin as soon as possible.

I am looking forward to hearing from you. Enclosed is my resume.

Sincerely,


Laura M. Page
(317) 555-6212

Anthony H. Cohen
167 Tuxedo Drive
Redding, CT 06896
(203) 555-1678

February 8, 1993

Mr. George Smart
Director of Personnel
Vocational Technical College
8775 West Douglas Street
Virginia Beach, VA 23456

Dear Mr. Smart:

For the past ten years, I have had a rewarding career with Central State Hospital in Connecticut. I now find myself ready to take on a new challenge as a teacher of mental health workers.

During my career at Central State Hospital, I have held positions as mental health counselor and director of psychiatric social work. Being part of the mental health community has shown me the great need for well-trained workers in this area.

I would like the opportunity to speak with you about my background and the potential areas where my expertise can be used to train mental health workers. A resume is enclosed that details my qualifications.

Sincerely yours,

Anthony H. Cohen

AHC/tbd

Enclosure

2234 Eden Hollow Road, Suite 5
New York, NY 10020
Office:    (212) 555-7788
Fax:       (212) 555-0098


August 27, 1992


John Boyd
The Far West Pharmaceutical Company
7722 Oakwood Drive
San Ramon, CA 94527

Dear John:

The progressive and innovative nature of The Far West Pharmaceutical
Company appeals to me.

I am looking for a position as a salesperson with a pharmaceutical house
after spending the past five years as a pharmacist in a retail store.

A resume is enclosed that describes my experience and qualifications.  I
look forward to hearing from you soon to set up an appointment for an
interview.

Please keep all contact personal and confidential.


Sincerely,


Michael K. Smith

October 18, 1992

Human Resources
8825 North Woodland Drive
Council Bluffs, Iowa 51503

To whom it may concern:

I am writing to inquire about any openings you may have for clinical nurse specialists in geriatric medicine.  My experience in geriatric nursing includes working in the Alzheimer's unit of Memorial Hospital and the Oak Brook Nursing Home.

Recently, I completed a Gerontological Nurse Practitioner training program.  In addition, I hold gerontology certification.

If you should have an interest in further discussing my qualifications, please contact me at (712) 555-0134.  My resume is enclosed for your review.

Sincerely,


David Allen Connors
5578 Douglas Drive
Council Bluffs, Iowa 51504

Charles D. Stiles

6225 High Drive, New Brunswick, NJ 08901

October 8, 1992

Human Resources Department
Clear Laboratories
13 Aspen Drive
Trenton, NJ 06902

Dear Sir/Madam:

I am writing to you with the hope that you might have an opening soon in your laboratory for a medical technologist. If you do not, I would appreciate your keeping my resume on file for future opportunities.

My course work for a master's degree in medical technology was recently completed at Johns Hopkins University. Presently, I am writing a report for my research project in microbiology.

I am a sincere, hard-working individual with the ability to learn quickly. I enjoy challenging work and am capable of working under pressure.

Thank you for taking the time to consider my qualifications and candidacy. I look forward to hearing from you soon.

Sincerely Yours,

Charles D. Stiles
(201) 555-2609

Enclosure

3345 Lucas Street
Dallas, TX 75235


January 19, 1993


Personnel Director
Washington Township School Corporation
Lindenwood Ave.
Austin, TX 78768

Dear Personnel Director:

I am writing to obtain further information regarding employment with your school corporation as a school nurse.

I read about your corporation in *The Texan State Journal* and would like to inquire about career opportunities within your school district.

I will be graduating from SMU in May of this year with a Bachelor of Science degree in nursing. Throughout my collegiate career, I have maintained a balanced background of activities and academics. In addition, my summer internship provided me with invaluable work experience in the emergency room of Kennedy Hospital.

A copy of my resume is enclosed for your review. If you need further information, I will be more than happy to provide you with the necessary materials.

I know how busy you must be during this time of year, but I would appreciate a few minutes of your time. I may be reached at the above address or by calling (214) 555-2203. I look forward to hearing from you about my future with your school corporation.

Sincerely,


Maria P. Day


Enclosure: Resume

December 17, 1992

Ruth Fong
Pacific Press
255 Long Hill Rd.
Middletown, CT 06457

Dear Ms. Fong:

I wish to apply for a position as a medical illustrator with Pacific Press. I hold an undergraduate degree in biology and a master's degree in medical illustration. In addition, I am a member of the Association of Medical Illustrators. I have an extensive and varied background working on ophthalmology drawings as well as with educators and authors. This experience, combined with my schooling and personal interest in illustrating, could be very valuable to your company.

Enclosed is my resume. I am willing to relocate. Please feel free to call me and set up an interview at your convenience.

Sincerely,


Jerome Palmer
5544 Wildwood Drive
West Lake, Ohio 44145
(614) 555-4014

2556 Forest St.
Houston, TX  77063
January 27, 1993


Personnel Director
Valley Hospital
P. O. Box 228964
Birmingham, AL 35222-8964

Dear Personnel Director:

Please consider my application for a position as a dietitian.  I graduated from Purdue University with a Bachelor of Science degree in dietetics.  I have been a registered dietitian for the past three years.

I feel that my experience as a dietitian in a nursing home and clinic, along with my education, qualifies me for a position with Valley Hospital.  I will continue to be successful as a dietitian because I enjoy the challenge of helping people regain their health through proper diet.  Furthermore, I work hard and am concerned with doing my best at all times.

I would like to have an interview to discuss how my placement with your hospital would benefit both of us.  Please phone me any time at (713) 555-8866.  I look forward to hearing from you.

Yours truly,



Edda Fisher



Enclosure

November 20, 1992
1516 North Central Ave.
Indianapolis, IN 46208


Dr. James Day
Clay Hospital
9888 West Washington Blvd.
Indianapolis, IN 46208

Dear Dr. Day:

This letter is in reply to the advertisement in the *Indianapolis Star* on Sunday, November 19.

I earned a degree in musical therapy from Indiana University in May of this year. Recently, I completed an internship at Coleman Hospital in Indianapolis where I worked with severely retarded children. I play the piano, guitar, violin, and recorder and enjoy using folk music as a part of my treatment therapy. I have attached a qualifications summary and other pertinent data for your consideration.

I think that my experiences can be utilized by Clay Hospital to your advantage, and I look forward to an interview with you.


Sincerely,


Kathy Johnson
(317) 555-3953

JILL R. McCOY
473 HILL DRIVE WEST
LINCOLNWOOD, IL 60646
(708) 555-6320


March 13, 1993


Ms. Julia Serafini
Crestwood Manor
6341 Crestwood Dr.
Naperville, IL 60565

Dear Ms. Serafini:

I will be graduating from Northwestern University in May. I am seeking a position as an occupational therapist in a nursing home setting.

My education at Northwestern University exposed me to the latest developments in occupational therapy. It also provided me with the opportunity to work with individuals in retirement communities, senior citizen centers, and rehabilitation centers. In addition, I have enhanced my education with extra courses in gerontology.

Enclosed, you will find my resume. A complete credentials file is available upon request through Northwestern University; Educational Placement Office; 4600 S. Main Street; Evanston, IL 60043; 708/555-9987.

I would like to request an interview with Crestwood Manor. I may be contacted at the above number.

Sincerely,


Jill R. McCoy

Enclosure

Elizabeth A. Grossa
1346 E. 22nd St. #105
Chicago, IL 60302

January 8, 1993

Optics Plus
8465 Baker Street
Chicago, IL 60302

To Whom It May Concern:

This letter is in response to the Optics Plus ad placed in the *Chicago Tribune* on January 7, 1993.

I have a master in ophthalmic optics certificate and hold an Illinois license to dispense eyeglasses. I have worked in an hospital eye clinic for seven years and would now like to work in a retail optical store. Your ad was of particular interest to me as the job is for a position in the Chicago area.

My experience in the hospital environment has provided me with the opportunity to handle a wide variety of vision needs. Besides being a skilled optician, I have been told that my communication skills are excellent.

Enclosed is my resume detailing my work experience, certification, and educational background. I feel that my qualifications would be an asset to your corporation.

I would welcome the opportunity for a personal interview to discuss the position at Optics Plus.

Sincerely,

Elizabeth A. Grossa

## GEORGE LONG

### 655 Kelton Avenue, Los Angeles, CA 90024
### 310/555-9542

December 4, 1992

Anita Johnson
Los Angeles Drug Company
500 South Summit Drive
Burbank, CA   91523

Dear Ms. Johnson:

Please accept this letter as an application for the position of manager of the prescription department in the Burbank branch of the Los Angeles Drug Company.  I have enclosed a copy of my resume for your review.

Through my present employment as a pharmacist with Goldman Drugs, I have gained firsthand experience in merchandising, advertising, purchasing stock, and the supervision of pharmacists and clerks.  My formal education also includes an undergraduate degree in business.  Furthermore, I possess the people-oriented skills and strong professional background which this position requires.

I would very much like to further discuss my qualifications in an interview.

Sincerely,


George Long

JOANNE POWERS
95 LOWELL DRIVE, KALAMAZOO, MI 49001
(616) 555-4889

DECEMBER 9, 1993

Dr. Charlene Dixon
Kraft Medical Center
1000 Campus Drive
Kalamazoo, MI 49002

Dear Dr. Dixon:

I am responding to your advertisement in last Friday's
<u>Gazette</u>. I am interested in a full-time position as a
receptionist/secretary in your office.

Presently, I am working as a secretary in the office of
Dr. Charles Williams, who will be retiring at the end
of this month. My experience with Dr. Williams has
included billing, data entry, patient scheduling,
copying, filing, and handling collections on patient
accounts.

I am a self-starter who is resourceful, outgoing,
efficient, service-oriented, and extremely organized.
Superior recommendations are available from my
current employer.

I look forward to hearing from you in the near future
to schedule an interview.

Yours truly,


Joanne Powers

enclosure

ANGELA CASTLE

225 Landon Drive, Ionia, Michigan 48846
(616) 555-1053


November 12, 1992



Ralph Jansen, D.D.S.
1224 East Drive
Detroit, Michigan 48079

Dear Doctor Jansen,

Are you looking for someone who can:

* play a key role in patient care?

* work with children and adults in a gentle and caring
  manner?

* effectively handle emergencies?

* offer recent training from seminars in restoration,
  dental implants, nitrous oxide sedation, cosmetic
  bonding, and bleaching?

* work on evenings and Saturdays?

In the ten years that I have worked as a dental assistant, I
have assisted dentists in general dentistry as well as
handled billing and appointments. In addition, I have
experience with computer aided dentistry. My experience has
taught me the importance of good people skills and keeping
abreast of the most recent technogical advances in dentistry.

I look forward to the opportunity to meet with you personally
to discuss my qualifications as a dental assistant. You may
contact me in the evenings at the above telephone number.

Very truly yours,



Angela Castle

enclosure

19 East 83rd Street Apt. 32
New York, New York 10024
(212) 555-5626

May 21, 1993

Ms. Linda Lansing
Director, Human Resources
New York General Hospital
78 Lexington Avenue
New York, New York 10028

Dear Ms. Lansing:

Please accept this letter and my resume as an application for a position on the New York General Hospital staff. If you are looking for a compassionate hard-working professional who is willing to put in long hours, I believe I can make a positive contribution to your hospital.

As you may note in my resume, I have recently completed my residency at Walter Reed Hospital in Washington, D.C. During my time at Walter Reed, I also worked as a volunteer three nights a week for the Homeless Help Program. Through my volunteer activities, I have gained experience working with a vast number of individuals of various ages and socioeconomic backgrounds.

Besides solid medical skills, you will find that I have exceptionally strong organizational skills and am able to work independently with little or no supervision. I am looking for a hospital where I can best utilize my personal and professional skills, and satisfy my desire to serve humanity.

Should my qualifications meet the needs of your hospital, I would appreciate the opportunity for a personal interview at your earliest convenience. If you should need any additional information regarding my qualifications, please do not hesitate to contact me anytime.

Thank you for your time and consideration. I look forward to talking with you in the very near future.

Sincerely,


Michael R. Crowe

Encl: Resume, References

Stephanie Kohl
3412 York Avenue South
Chicago, IL 61646
(213) 555-6321


January 23, 1993


Ms. Claudia Brown
Human Resources Director
Bloomington Consolidated School District
Bloomington, MN 55347

Dear Ms. Brown:

I am seeking a position as a speech language/pathologist in
an elementary school setting and looking forward to
relocating to the Greater Minneapolis area.

I received my Master's degree in speech language/pathology
from the University of Minnesota and hold state licenses in
Illinois and Minnesota.  My experience includes working in
public elementary and secondary schools as well as at a
county school for the hearing impaired.  In addition, I sign
fluently.

Enclosed is a resume to assist you in evaluating my
qualifications.  If you need further information, please do
not hesitate to contact me.

I will look forward to the opportunity to meet with you to
discuss my qualifications for employment in your school
district.  Thank you for your consideration.

Sincerely,



Stephanie Kohl

# VGM CAREER BOOKS

**CAREER DIRECTORIES**
Careers Encyclopedia
Dictionary of Occupational Titles
Occupational Outlook Handbook

**CAREERS FOR**
Animal Lovers
Bookworms
Computer Buffs
Crafty People
Culture Lovers
Environmental Types
Film Buffs
Foreign Language Aficionados
Good Samaritans
Gourmets
History Buffs
Kids at Heart
Nature Lovers
Night Owls
Number Crunchers
Shutterbugs
Sports Nuts
Travel Buffs

**CAREERS IN**
Accounting; Advertising; Business; Child
Care; Communications; Computers;
Education; Engineering; Finance;
Government; Health Care; High Tech;
Journalism; Law; Marketing; Medicine;
Science; Social & Rehabilitation Services

**CAREER PLANNING**
Admissions Guide to Selective
    Business Schools
Beginning Entrepreneur
Career Planning & Development for
    College Students & Recent Graduates
Career Change
Careers Checklists
Cover Letters They Don't Forget
Executive Job Search Strategies
Guide to Basic Cover Letter Writing
Guide to Basic Resume Writing
Joyce Lain Kennedy's Career book
Out of Uniform
Slam Dunk Resumes
Successful Interviewing for College
    Seniors

**CAREER PORTRAITS**
Animals
Music
Sports
Teaching

**GREAT JOBS FOR**
English Majors
Foreign Language Majors
History Majors
Psychology Majors

**HOW TO**
Approach an Advertising Agency and
    Walk Away with the Job You Want
Bounce Back Quickly After
    Losing Your Job
Change Your Career
Choose the Right Career
Find Your New Career Upon Retirement
Get & Keep Your First Job
Get Hired Today
Get into the Right Law School
Have a Winning Job Interview
Hit the Ground Running in Your New Job
Improve Your Study Skills
Jump Start a Stalled Career
Land a Better Job
Launch Your Career in TV News
Make the Right Career Moves
Market Your College Degree
Move from College into a
    Secure Job
Negotiate the Raise
    You Deserve
Prepare a *Curriculum Vitae*

Prepare for College
Run Your Own Home Business
Succeed in College
Succeed in High School
Write a Winning Resume
Write Successful Cover Letters
Write Term Papers & Reports
Write Your College
    Application Essay

**OPPORTUNITIES IN**
Accounting
Acting
Advertising
Aerospace
Agriculture
Airline
Animal & Pet Care
Architecture
Automotive Service
Banking
Beauty Culture
Biological Sciences
Biotechnology
Book Publishing
Broadcasting
Building Construction Trades
Business Communication
Business Management
Cable Television
CAD/CAM
Carpentry
Chemistry
Child Care
Chiropractic
Civil Engineering
Cleaning Service
Commercial Art & Graphic Design
Computer Maintenance
Computer Science
Counseling & Development
Crafts
Culinary
Customer Service
Data Processing
Dental Care
Desktop Publishing
Direct Marketing
Drafting
Electrical Trades
Electronics
Energy
Engineering
Engineering Technology
Environmental
Eye Care
Fashion
Fast Food
Federal Government
Film
Financial
Fire Protection Services
Fitness
Food Services
Foreign Language
Forestry
Health & Medical
High Tech
Home Economics
Homecare Services
Horticulture
Hospital Administration
Hotel & Motel Management
Human Resource Management
Information Systems
Installation & Repair
Insurance
Interior Design
International Business
Journalism
Laser Technology
Law
Law Enforcement & Criminal
    Justice
Library & Information Science
Machine Trades
Magazine Publishing

Marine & Maritime
Marketing
Masonry
Medical Imaging
Medical Technology
Metalworking
Military
Modeling
Music
Newspaper Publishing
Nonprofit Organizations
Nursing
Nutrition
Occupational Therapy
Office Occupations
Paralegal
Paramedical
Part-time & Summer Jobs
Performing Arts
Petroleum
Pharmacy
Photography
Physical Therapy
Physician
Physician Assistant
Plastics
Plumbing & Pipe Fitting
Postal Service
Printing
Property Management
Psychology
Public Health
Public Relations
Purchasing
Real Estate
Recreation & Leisure
Refrigeration & Air Conditioning
Religious Service
Restaurant
Retailing
Robotics
Sales
Secretarial
Social Science
Social Work
Speech-Language Pathology
Sports & Athletics
Sports Medicine
State & Local Government
Teaching
Technical Writing & Communications
Telecommunications
Telemarketing
Television & Video
Theatrical Design & Production
Tool & Die
Transportation
Travel
Trucking
Veterinary Medicine
Visual Arts
Vocational & Technical
Warehousing
Waste Management
Welding
Word Processing
Writing
Your Own Service Business

**RESUMES FOR**
Advertising Careers
Banking and Financial Careers
Business Management Careers
College Students &
    Recent Graduates
Communications Careers
Education Careers
Engineering Careers
Environmental Careers
Health and Medical Careers
High School Graduates
High Tech Careers
Midcareer Job Changes
Sales and Marketing Careers
Scientific and Technical Careers
Social Service Careers
The First-Time Job Hunter

**VGM Career Horizons**
a division of *NTC Publishing Group*
4255 West Touhy Avenue
Lincolnwood, Illinois 60646–1975